East Asia at a Crossroads

The Japan Center for International Exchange wishes to thank

Asia Pacific Agenda Project

East Asia at a Crossroads

Edited by

Jusuf Wanandi and Tadashi Yamamoto

Japan Center for International Exchange
Tokyo • New York

Japanese names in this book are in given name–surname order; all other names
are treated according to country practice.

Copyediting by Kimberly Gould Ashizawa and Susan Hubbard.
Cover and typographic design by Patrick Ishiyama.

Printed in Japan.
ISBN 4-88907-078-8

Distributed outside Japan by Brookings Institution Press (1775 Massachusetts
Avenue, NW, Washington DC 20036-2188 USA) and Kinokuniya Company Ltd.
(5-38-1 Sakuragaoka, Setagaya-ku, Tokyo 156-8691 Japan).

Japan Center for International Exchange
4-9-17 Minami Azabu, Minato-ku, Tokyo 106-0047 Japan
URL: www.jcie.or.jp

Japan Center for International Exchange, Inc. (JCIE/USA)
274 Madison Avenue, Suite 1102, New York NY 10016 USA
URL: www.jcie.org

Contents

Foreword

East Asian efforts to build the underpinnings of a regional community have drawn heightened attention in recent years. In a sense, the push to establish regional institutions and mechanisms has been a natural outgrowth of the region's rapidly growing economic interdependence. At another level, these efforts also reflect an acknowledgement of the need for greater regional cooperation in the face of growing transnational challenges, as well as a calculation that strengthening regional institutions can help stabilize East Asia in a period of dynamic change and shifting balances of power.

Despite the notable progress made to date, the question remains as to how much further community building can proceed in the face of the mutual suspicions, deepset animosities, and widespread disparities that persist among states in the region. In a sense, East Asia finds itself at a crossroads, where regional cooperation can help overcome these divisions or where it can fall victim to them. With this in mind, the contributors to this study attempt to assess the current state of East Asia community building and identify ways that momentum can be sustained and regional cooperation further deepened. At the same time, they examine an issue that is often overlooked in the debate about regionalism in East Asia, namely how a more coherent East Asia might be a better global citizen. In other words, they are concerned with how regional community might better enable East Asia to serve as a counterpart for interregional initiatives, primarily with Europe and North America, and how it can ultimately provide a platform for East Asia to expand its contributions to global governance.

This study was undertaken under the auspices of the Asia Pacific Agenda Project (APAP), an initiative operated by a consortium of policy research institutions that promote joint policy research, dialogue, and information sharing on key issues facing the Asia Pacific. With the Japan Center for International Exchange (JCIE) serving as the secretariat for APAP, leading intellectual figures from around East Asia—including from China, Japan, Indonesia, and the Philippines—as well as from Europe and North America were convened for two forums, the first in Bali, Indonesia, on November 27–28, 2006, and the second in Tokyo, Japan, on March 10–11, 2007. All of this was made possible by the generous funding of Japan's Ministry of Foreign Affairs.

The book that emerged from these discussions has been brought to fruition through the hard work of the staff of JCIE in cooperation with their counterparts in the APAP member institutions. While extending our deep gratitude to all of them, we would like to particularly note the efforts of Ryo Sahashi and Hyoma Ito to help organize the workshops; the work of Hideko Katsumata, James Gannon, and Ryo Sahashi to shepherd this book to completion; the able copyediting of Kim Ashizawa and Susan Hubbard; and the layout and design of Patrick Ishiyama. Most of all, we wish to thank the authors, who have been so generous with their time and so willing to engage intellectually on this important topic.

In an era when East Asia is becoming an increasingly important player in global affairs, we hope that this study can help deepen understanding of what is actually underway at the regional level and perhaps provoke greater exploration of how East Asia might contribute more effectively to the international community.

TADASHI YAMAMOTO   JUSUF WANANDI

List of Abbreviations

APEC	Asia Pacific Economic Cooperation
ARF	ASEAN Regional Forum
ASEAN	Association of Southeast Asian Nations
ASEAN+3	ASEAN countries plus China, Japan, and South Korea
ASEAN+6	ASEAN+3 plus Australia, India, and New Zealand
ASEM	Asia-Europe Meeting
CLMV	Cambodia, Lao PDR, Myanmar, and Vietnam
CSO	Civil society organization
EAFTA	East Asian Free Trade Agreement
EASG	East Asia Study Group
EAVG	East Asia Vision Group
EEC	European Economic Community
EU	European Union
FDI	Foreign direct investment
FTA	Free trade agreement
FTAAP	Free Trade Area of the Asia Pacific
G-8	Group of Eight
GDI	Gender-Related Development Index
GDP	Gross domestic product
HDI	Human Development Index
KEDO	Korean Peninsula Energy Development Organization
NAFTA	North American Free Trade Agreement
NATO	North Atlantic Treaty Organization
NGO	Nongovernmental organization
NPT	Nonproliferation Treaty
ODA	Official development assistance
OECD	Organisation for Economic Cooperation and Development
OSCE	Organization for Security Cooperation in Europe
PPP	Purchasing power parity
PSI	Proliferation Security Initiative
ROK	Republic of Korea (South Korea)
SAR	Special Administrative Region (Hong Kong SAR)
SARS	Severe acute respiratory syndrome
UN	United Nations
UNDP	United Nations Development Programme
WTO	World Trade Organization

I

Overview

1

East Asia at a Crossroads

Tadashi Yamamoto and James Gannon

Ten years have passed since the Asian economic crisis exposed the dark side of the region's growing interdependence. Since then, the region's economies and wellbeing have only become more interconnected, and regional leaders have embarked on a drive to build up a framework for greater regional cooperation and integration under the rubric of an East Asia community. This is not an entirely new movement; there have been a series of halting efforts to construct some sort of regional community since at least the 1960s. However, there has been a palpable feeling that these efforts have been infused with a greater sense of purpose over the last decade. The result has been the emergence of a complex set of overlapping multilateral forums and mechanisms in the region, complemented by a growing web of bilateral economic agreements.

While many of these arrangements are still nonbinding and fragile, they present a historic opportunity to reshape the region to better deal with the increasingly complex realities of an interconnected world and, hopefully, propel it toward a future in which war might be as unthinkable as it is today in Europe. In a sense, East Asia community building is now at a historic crossroads, where it can be further advanced and deepened or where it can succumb to the many disparities and emerging rivalries that characterize this rapidly changing region.

In this volume, leading experts from around East Asia, as well as from Europe and North America, analyze the dynamics of regional community building, which they agree is still at a beginning stage. As they note, this round of community building started in Southeast Asia and has spread outward. In the mid- to late-1990s, ASEAN expanded to include all of the countries in Southeast Asia, and in December 1997, half a year after the onset of the economic crisis, the heads of government from China, Japan, and Korea gathered with leaders of ASEAN's member countries along the sidelines of the annual ASEAN summit for what would be the first ASEAN+3 leaders meeting. In the ensuing years, its meetings have become regularized and ASEAN+3 has started to serve as an umbrella for a range of cooperative mechanisms in the fields of finance, trade, and cross-border "functional issues."

In 1998, the ASEAN+3 leaders established the East Asia Vision Group (EAVG) to develop a set of proposals for regional cooperation, and these recommendations were then debated by a committee of ASEAN+3 government representatives meeting as the East Asia Study Group (EASG). When it wound up its deliberations in 2002, the EASG selected 26 concrete proposals for priority, ranging from the promotion of nongovernmental networks and exchanges in the region to the establishment of an East Asia free trade area.

The process of building regional institutions was unexpectedly accelerated by the political maneuvering that led to the launch of the East Asia Summit in December 2005, which had been cited only as a long-term objective in the EASG final report. This new summit gained widespread attention, even if it was lacking in clearly delineated objectives, and nations outside of East Asia, such as Australia, India, and New Zealand, scrambled to be included.

The result has been two institutional tracks for regional community building: a narrow ASEAN+3 and the more expansive East Asia Summit. On the ground, though, the picture has been further complicated by the rapid proliferation of bilateral and multilateral economic partnership agreements and free trade agreements throughout the region, as well as the evolution of the Six-Party Talks into a more regularized forum in Northeast Asia. Meanwhile, however, over the course of the decade since the 1997 economic crisis that many came to associate with American detachment from the region, the track record for broadly gauged multilateral forums linking the world's one superpower—the United States—to the region has been mixed at best. One broader forum, the ASEAN Regional Forum (ARF), which involves the United States, the European Union, Russia, and 23 other countries, has become a useful discussion forum on regional security issues. However, APEC, the main multilateral institution linking the United States with East Asia, has lost a great deal of its momentum.

The Nature of East Asia Community Building

Underlying these varied efforts is a sense that it is important to forge a regional community not only to better reflect the economic integration that has been proceeding on its own but also to help manage the seismic shifts that are now underway in terms of the regional and global balance of power. In this volume's second chapter, Jusuf Wanandi places the community-building process in a historical context by explaining that, provided its economic ascendance continues, it is likely that East Asia "will indeed become the most important region of the globe" and that the balance of power between the United States, Europe, and Asia is bound to tip in the middle of this century, first in terms of economics and then perhaps politics and security. The uncertainties surrounding this power shift are intensified by rivalries within East Asia among regional powers, particularly China and Japan, and by the declining regional influence of a distracted United States. In essence, we seem to be witnessing simultaneous shifts in both the global balance of power and the regional balance of power.

Such shifts tend to breed instability, and history warns that economic dynamism is often not enough to forestall conflict. The experience of Europe in the late 19th century and first half of the 20th century, until the European powers were drawn into an economic and security community, is an object lesson in this regard. One of the overarching rationales for East Asia community building is thus to help ease this transition by "complementing the new balance of power in East Asia and strengthening the stakes that every country has in preserving peace and stability in the future."

Of course, this regional community has to develop in a manner befitting East Asia's unique circumstances rather than along the path that Europe has successfully taken. As Wanandi notes, community-building efforts in the region are by necessity a work in progress. Realities on the ground dictate that, for the time being, cooperation can only move forward easily in certain areas—for example, on economics and "functional issues"—and it is much more difficult where issues of sovereignty come into play. Meanwhile, the stakes that East Asia has in the global economy, as well as in the broader international system, compel it to pursue a very open form of regionalism rather than build up walls to the outside world.

These efforts to embed East Asia's powers into a stable and cooperative regional order have to overcome an imposing set of obstacles, which are adeptly analyzed by Carolina Hernandez in the following chapter. She breaks these down into three categories: structural and historical, political, and socioeconomic obstacles. The most acute of the structural and historical obstacles involves the major powers in the region—China and Japan—which are potential rivals whose relations both with each other and with other countries in the region are tainted by lingering historical animosities. An intensified competition for regional predominance between these two countries has the potential to unravel many of the gains made to date in terms of East Asia community building.

The political obstacles to community-building efforts are equally pressing, ranging from the difficulty in finding effective leadership for the regional community-building project to the region's diversity in terms of political systems and the difficulty East Asian governments have in mobilizing domestic political support for an East Asia community. Hernandez makes the case that ASEAN needs to be in the driver's seat for any regional community-building effort because neither China nor Japan can accede to the other's leadership. But internal dynamics in ASEAN itself make this challenging. Moreover, visionary personal leadership is still lacking; the fact is that "the region does not have the equivalent of a Monnet or a Schumann, who so successfully advocated the creation of a European Community."

Hernandez reminds us that socioeconomic obstacles also cannot be overlooked, especially since they are closely interconnected with the structural and political obstacles. The stark differences within the region in levels of economic development, say between Japan and Lao PDR, are much wider than any seen in Western Europe when it started on its drive to build a regional community. Therefore, sustainable community building requires concerted efforts to narrow regional disparities in terms of human development by working on poverty, health, education, and other issues affecting the living conditions of the broad mass of East Asia's populace because "community, in the final analysis, is about people."

In the eyes of Qin Yaqing, these obstacles are ultimately rooted in the basic tensions concerning sovereignty and the role of nation-states in a globalized world. He argues that the key challenge to regional community building is the difficulty that East Asia faces in overcoming its Westphalian culture, or at least in reducing its intensity. Every nation in East Asia is highly sensitive to issues involving national sovereignty, yet regional cooperation is urgently needed, and not only in terms of economics but also to sufficiently meet the region's growing number of nontraditional security challenges—running the gamut from communicable disease and environmental degradation to terrorism and transnational crime.

Therefore, Qin asserts that moving forward on regional community building requires facing up to the limitations that the current Westphalian culture places on regional cooperation. It is natural for there to be numerous disagreements about the potential shape of an East Asia community and how it should be built. In the face of these limitations, it is important to accept that this Westphalian culture cannot be changed overnight and that the key to success is to "amass sufficient political will to at least maintain the momentum of regional cooperation and integration."

In order to do this, Qin offers several recommendations that go to the heart of the nature of the East Asia community-building process. For one, it is important to recognize that, at this stage of community building, process is often more important than results since it is necessary to build habits of cooperation. In other words, "once nations are involved in the process, they are integrating and being integrated." A continued emphasis on economics is key, since progress in this area is one of the most effective ways to push forward the regional process. Special care needs to be taken to avoid exacerbating major power rivalries in the region, particularly between China and Japan, by refraining from using community building as a tool to balance one another's influence and avoiding situations that encourage China and Japan to compete for regional leadership in the community-building process. And there is a need for greater efforts to build public awareness and popular support for regional community building among the region's citizens if the process is to be sustainable, for East Asia community building "cannot be an elite program forever." The key to progress on all of these points, he argues, is the demonstration of strong political will on the part of the region's leaders.

A Vision for Moving Forward

The study's authors generally agree that a gradual, step-by-step process of expanding cooperation is the most effective way of moving forward the regional community-building process right now. In his chapter, Wanandi maps out one possible institutional framework for regional integration that can bring some order to the region's overlapping forums and mechanisms while better reflecting the actual balance of power in the region. He proposes that the East Asia Summit be converted into a kind of East Asia G-8, a concert of powers for the region that serves as a forum for discussing high-order strategic issues. For this to succeed, the inclusion of the United States in the East Asia Summit is integral. Meanwhile, in his view, ASEAN+3 should be the main institution for deepening economic and functional cooperation in the region, although it can still involve outside countries such as Australia and the United States on a case-by-case basis when tackling individual issues. Political realities necessitate that ASEAN remain in the "driver's seat" of regional community-building efforts for the time being, which means that ASEAN must find ways to strengthen its internal capacity. At the same time, the ARF can serve as an important vehicle for confidence-building measures and initiatives in the area of nontraditional security.

The authors of three other chapters call for deeper regional cooperation in particular issue areas. Jesus Estanislao argues that there are numerous opportunities for deeper cooperation in the field of economics that remain untapped. Considerable attention has been paid to the flurry of bilateral trade agreements recently forged between economies in the region, and there is a need for greater regional efforts to harmonize the wide array of conflicting rules associated with these. He also proposes regional initiatives to promote innovation by deepening exchanges of knowledge and technology through greater cooperation between research institutes and universities in the region. And he argues that regional financial cooperation should go beyond the limited steps we have seen so far to include joint work on risk management and greater efforts to strengthen the region's corporate bond markets. Combined, these steps can improve the conditions for what he describes as the market trinity of trade, innovation, and finance.

However, Estanislao also makes the case that there is a need to broaden the regional economic agenda beyond these areas. In light of East Asia's rapid urbanization, there is a growing need to continue improving public governance in a farsighted manner so as to make the region's cities more livable and economically competitive. Meanwhile, steps need to be taken, particularly in terms of education, skills training, and social services delivery, to respond to rising income inequality. Also, it is important to continue to support the transition toward the rule of law that has been underway throughout East Asia in order to meet the challenges that corruption poses to the workings of the region's increasingly free and open markets. In Estanislao's eyes, these needs make a compelling case for prioritizing governance issues on the regional community-building agenda.

Rizal Sukma, meanwhile, focuses on the many opportunities for deeper cooperation on nontraditional security, particularly through the introduction of human security approaches to the growing number of cross-border problems in the region. States in East Asia face a widening array of human security threats—ranging from environmental degradation to piracy and transnational crime—and these can only be effectively countered through regional cooperation. By and large, East Asian leaders are increasingly receptive to efforts in the field of human security, which recognize the interconnectedness of the various causes of insecurity in peoples' lives and endeavor to protect them and empower them to better respond to these challenges. This, Sukma argues, leaves the region ripe for the mainstreaming of human security approaches and their institutionalization as a key component of the regional community-building effort. In the end, concerted joint initiatives to face these challenges would help build up habits of cooperation in a region characterized by insufficient mutual trust and low levels of institutionalization, and this can have positive spillover effects that add momentum to the broader community-building project.

Meanwhile, Hitoshi Tanaka, writing with Adam P. Liff, echoes Sukma's calls for greater cooperation on nontraditional security issues by proposing the establishment of an "East Asia Security Forum," which would focus on common threats such as piracy, terrorism, and communicable disease. This would be designed to supplement a regional security regime that, for the foreseeable future, should continue to necessitate active US involvement and be underpinned by the web of US alliances and security guarantees in the region.

Instead of just promoting dialogue on security issues, as the ARF currently does, an East Asia Security Forum would be designed to take specific, proactive steps to respond to nontraditional security threats and, as states in the region become accustomed to working together, the institution's mandate could be gradually expanded to deal with threats that are more traditional in nature. They believe that in a region divided by the rise of nationalistic sentiments and a lack of common values, participation in rules-based institutions such as this forum and the other institutions that undergird an East Asia community would play an integral role in cultivating the trust, confidence, and interdependency that is needed to avoid an intensification of great-power rivalry.

East Asia Community in the Global Context

In the volume's final section, two authors from outside of the region, one from the United States and one from Germany, assess efforts to build regional community from a global perspective. Writing on the basis of his experience on Capitol Hill, Frank Jannuzi concludes that the deep-set resistance found in US policy circles to regional community-building initiatives is starting to soften, although American leaders continue to harbor considerable skepticism and are not prepared to invest heavily in new, untested regional organizations. He argues that it appears that "as time goes by, the United States seems poised to embrace regionalism in East Asia, first as part of a mixed strategy and perhaps eventually as a genuine alternative to the bilateral alliances forged during the Cold War." This shift is likely to be driven by a growing sense that although the American hub-and-spokes system of bilateral alliances needs to be maintained as the backbone of any US approach to the region, a narrow reliance on bilateral ties alone is increasingly out of touch with regional realities and the preponderance of new transnational security challenges. Instead, so long as the community remains an open one, US interests can be better served over the long term by the emergence of a regional community that can play a meaningful role in responding to transnational challenges and stabilizing the region, even if the United States is not a formal member. This means that it is likely that future US administrations will be increasingly inclined to play a more active and supportive role in regional forums, if only to ensure that US leadership is not diminished in a rapidly changing region.

Meanwhile, Karl Kaiser's closing chapter goes to the heart of one overarching question inspiring this volume—how regional community building can contribute to better governance. He notes several ways in which regionalism helps improve governance in and among participating countries. The development of regional cooperation enhances states' capacity to better manage the type of heightened economic interdependence that is so prominent in East Asia, and it helps them respond more effectively to transnational problems and common domestic challenges. Ultimately, successful integration should help advance regional peace and stability through the creation of shared interests in preventing political crises from getting out of hand.

Kaiser explains that regionalism does not just help improve regional governance; it also can make important contributions to global governance. The most difficult challenges facing the world today tend to be those that cross national boundaries, such as terrorism, the proliferation of weapons of mass destruction, and global warming. Effectively responding to these issues requires multilateral action and global cooperation, and interregional cooperation is one important component of these responses. The development of regional institutions is crucial in this context because it can facilitate interregional cooperation and support global initiatives by mobilizing regional consensus and providing focal points for regions to interact with one another. In the end, stronger regional community in East Asia can provide a firmer platform for Asia-Europe and Asia–North America cooperation on key global issues.

East Asia at a Crossroads

The changes unfolding at the regional level and the region's increasing weight in global affairs have brought East Asia to a crossroads where cooperation can be advanced through greater regional community building or its momentum can dissipate in the face of a host of deeply rooted obstacles. All of the contributors to this volume recognize that there is a natural speed limit built into this process; East Asian states inhabit a Westphalian world where they are generally loathe to cede even limited degrees of sovereignty to regional institutions. Yet East Asia's leaders increasingly see the utility of binding one another into cooperative mechanisms in order to help decrease the prospects of regional instability and more effectively respond to a growing number of cross-border and regional challenges. In this context, it seems that the best way forward is through a sort of strategic functionalism that encourages the development of habits of cooperation in a gradually expanding number of key areas where states are willing to commit to regional action. The goal is to do this in a way that feeds a virtuous cycle that can ultimately strengthen the institutional framework of the regional order.

In the end, it is also important to recognize that a central aim of East Asia community building should be to contribute to better governance. Moves to build cooperation on a range of noncontroversial issues should help improve governance at the regional level, not just by continuing to encourage the consolidation of peace in the region but also by facilitating more effective responses to the challenges facing the people of the region. However, East Asia community building is not just about the region. With global power shifting toward East Asia, the region has a duty and obligation to take on a more active role in supporting global governance in cooperation with those outside of the region. It seems clear that the development of mechanisms to encourage regional cooperation can be one step to help strengthen global governance by enabling East Asia to participate more fully and effectively in responding to global challenges.

While the road toward a true East Asia community is bound to be an arduous and uncertain one, if handled well, the strengthening and institutionalization of regional cooperation should not only enhance peace, prosperity, and wellbeing among the states in the region but also enable East Asia as a whole to better live up to its growing responsibilities as a stakeholder in the international community.

II

East Asia
Community Building:
Progress and Obstacles

2

East Asian Regionalism and Global Governance

Jusuf Wanandi

The East Asian region has done well economically thanks to the active role of the private sector over the last two decades, but from the politico-security perspective, it is faced with uncertainties.

The role and presence of the US military in the East Asian region has been the anchor of peace and stability since World War II. While bilateral alliances—especially the US-Japan alliance—have been the main instrument for the US presence and are still in place (being dependent on the naval and air forces of the Seventh Fleet), the political attention and presence of the United States as the only global superpower and regional power has declined in relative terms.

The focus of the United States, which is capable of paying complete attention to only one big problem or crisis at a time, has been completely diverted to the conflict in the Middle East—especially Iraq and the Israeli-Palestinian conflict—as the situation and developments there remain fluid due to mistakes made by the Bush administration in its fight against global terrorism. As a result, its soft power has declined worldwide, including in East Asia.

This is not good for global stability and peace, and it is also not good for East Asia. The withdrawal of the United States from its role as the underpinning of the global and regional order will only open up uncertainty and instability as to who will try to fill in the vacuum and lacunas.

The mistakes made by the Bush administration will likely be corrected by a new Democratic administration, but it will take some time and many new policy reforms before full credibility and leadership will be restored. Thus, both support and criticism of the United States are essential. It must be encouraged to make changes and corrections to its policies and to the way in which it wields its influence—including in East Asia—in order to maintain peace, stability, and development in the region.

In the meantime, the region has seen new strategic developments and challenges that require some real responses. The most important and central element is the rise of China and how the region will cope with such a huge and powerful neighbor. Thus far, this rise has been a peaceful one.

Further along, in the medium term, there is also India's rise, which will similarly have an impact on East Asia. The South Asia subcontinent alone does not provide a large enough arena for India's increasing power, and India has always been attracted by the idea of getting involved in East Asia throughout recorded history.

Another strategic issue is the normalization of China-Japan relations, which is still being worked out between them with the support of the East Asian region. This is the first time in history that both countries are powerful, and therefore it is critical to the region that they find a way to peacefully coexist.

The most important issue for the region will be the future relationship between China and the United States. One is the only current superpower, and the other is a future one. How they relate to each other will determine the state of affairs in East Asia: peaceful or full of tensions with potential for conflicts. These major power issues are dealt with in the first section of this chapter.

The second section deals with the shift in the balance of power toward East Asia, starting in the economic realm, as well as the consequences of this shift and the importance of how it has happened. History has shown that this shift will not be an easy one. However, it is possible that it will occur peacefully, as happened in the early 20th century, when power shifted from the United Kingdom to the United States. The challenge arises if one accepts that there will be more than one great power in the middle of the 21st century, with the United States and China as the main candidates. Some *modus vivendi* will have to be found by both countries and by the region. The European experience of the 19th and 20th centuries has shown that economics alone is not adequate to keep peace and stability and that politics must also be handled correctly. This offers a good lesson for East Asia.

The third section looks at regional institution building in East Asia, which should play an important role in overcoming any conflicting shifts by complementing the new balance of power in East Asia and strengthening the stakes that every country has in preserving peace and stability in the future.

That is why it is so important that the United States also be a member in this regional institution. It also explains why ASEAN has a special role to play as a catalyst and as the occupant of the driver's seat, since the relations between the two big powers in the region (i.e., China and Japan) have not been normalized.

The fourth and final section focuses on the contribution of East Asia to global governance. East Asia should never be organized only for the region; it has always been an open region and has been thriving due to its open regionalism. In addition, with the shift of power toward East Asia, it is only natural that the region will have duties and obligations to support global governance and cannot enjoy a "free ride," which will no longer be acceptable to the international community. This section outlines some of the areas in which the region could effectively contribute.

The Major Powers in East Asia

In the early 1990s, following the bursting of its bubble economy, Japan entered a decade-long period of recession and deflation—a period that was prolonged by inadequate government policies, especially in the financial and banking sector. In the last few years, the economy has started to grow again, albeit slowly. But while Japan may have finally emerged from the recession, it still faces several constraints on its economy: the problems of demography and an aging society, inadequate productivity levels, low levels of foreign direct investment (FDI), rising poverty, and worsening income inequality. These are real issues that need to be tackled. It appears, however, that Japanese leaders have been paying a great deal of attention to foreign policy and security, as well as to social issues such as education, but have not focused enough on the economy—especially in terms of continuing Prime Minister Koizumi's economic reforms.

In the end, Japan's leaders may be forced to take action to address the country's lackluster growth and aging population (much like Koizumi did with the nonperforming loans) because these are issues that will place heavy financial pressures on the voters. Moreover, Japan's economic needs could intersect with the ambitious security goals of some of the country's recent leaders: Japan needs to be economically stronger if it is going to be able to play a more important role in East Asia.

Japan has felt compelled to do more to address political security issues because it understands the new strategic developments in the region. China's rise in East Asia is central, but there have been many other developments as well. East Asia has generally recovered from the economic crisis of 1997 and is becoming the most important economic region of the world. Meanwhile, the regional role of Japan's key ally, the United States, has shifted. America's attention has been diverted to the Middle East, and America's "soft power" in East Asia has declined somewhat because of its one-sided strategy toward the new threat of global terrorism. At the same time, the development of the North Korean nuclear weapons program and the increase in Chinese defense expenditures—the transparency of which is doubted—have placed Japan in a bind.

Japan has astutely decided to make use of the new global threat of terrorism to become a "normal" country with adequate defense capabilities and to implement its role within the context of its alliance with the United States. Japan has taken steps to strengthen its alliance with the United States but at the same time is trying to develop its own policies. This is especially true in terms of its stance on East Asia. Japan has been supporting the establishment of new regional institutions, with the long-term objective of creating an East Asia community. This objective is at the heart of Japan's Asia policy.

Japan is committed to the idea of regional cooperation and community building because it views it as a way to overcome the challenges posed by China. In the meantime, despite the challenges it faces, Japan is still the region's largest economy in terms of gross domestic product (GDP) and is very important to the region in terms of trade, investment, finance, and technology. As long as it gets its policies right, it will remain one of the most important members of the region.

Japan also began hedging its dealings with China by signing the Australia-Japan Joint Declaration on Security Cooperation in March 2007. This new security relationship should be balanced with Japan's commitment to East Asia community and should be transparent— particularly since Japan has been asking for transparency in terms of China's increased defense budget. Otherwise, Japan's intentions might be misunderstood, and the idea of an East Asia community might be jeopardized. Similarly, if not well explained, moves to promote the idea of an alliance of democracies in East Asia, consisting of the United States, Japan, Australia, and India, might also be misunderstood by China.

The rise of such a big country as China has been unprecedented in human history, as its economy has grown by 9.5 percent annually for the last 25 years. This type of growth was seen in some Western European countries in the 19th century, following the Industrial Revolution, and in Japan, Taiwan, and South Korea between the 1960s and the 1980s, but these are much smaller countries. Since 1978, China's GDP per capita has risen relative to that of the world leader, the United States, in almost exactly the same way that Japan's rose between 1950 and 1973, Taiwan's rose between 1958 and the late 1980s, and South Korea's rose between 1962 and the early 1990s. China's real income per capita has increased by 300 percent over this period. But China has achieved this from a much lower relative starting point. Today, China's income per capita relative to US levels is roughly where South Korea was in 1972, Taiwan was in 1966, and Japan was before 1950. For China, these are still the early days of the catching-up process.

India is even further behind on the "catching-up" curve since it began the process later than China. Relative to America's GDP per capita, India is where China was in 1986. Even in absolute terms, it is only where China was in 1993.

To appreciate the differences between India and China, one should look not only at their economic strategies, but also at their political development. Although both are the heirs to great civilizations, China's political development is inseparable from its state, while India's is insepa-rable from its social structure and, above all, from the role of the caste. India embraces the concept of "unity in diversity," while China follows the rule of a "unitary hard state," pursuing a single goal with determination and mobilizing the maximum resources toward its achievement.

China has largely replicated the growth pattern of other East Asian success stories, although its financial system remains weak and its economy more open to FDI than those of Japan and South Korea. Its growth is based on high savings, massive investment in infrastructure, universal basic education, rapid industrialization, an increasingly deregulated labor market, and an internationally open and competitive economy.

India's pattern of growth has been different—indeed, in many ways unique—as it has been service based. Savings are far lower than in China, as are its investments in infrastructure. India's industrialization is quite advanced, but this has developed under an import-substitution policy and still lacks competitiveness. The literacy rate is low, although elite education is well developed. India's formal labor market is among the most regulated in the world. Regulations and relatively high protection against imports continue to restrict competition in the domestic market.

China has accepted both growth and social transformation. India welcomes growth but tries to minimize social dislocations. The Chinese state sees development as both its goal and the foundation of its legitimacy. Chinese politics are developmental, while India's have remained predominantly patron-client in nature.

It is not difficult, therefore, to see why China's growth has been far higher than India's. China has not only saved and invested far more, it has exploited to a far greater degree the opportunities afforded by the global economy. Its population is also more skilled, while the social and economic transformation it has embraced is more profound.

China's development has been unprecedented because it has happened in a country with far more than a billion people. This made China the largest nation ever to experience such tremendous growth for a period of more than 25 years. And it has the potential to continue at the same pace for the next 20 to 30 years, depending on how it responds to new challenges or even calamities that it might face in the future.

That is why it could potentially become as large as the US economy in terms of purchasing power parity sometime around 2020, and could surpass the United States shortly thereafter. There might be corrections—economic and political—along the way, and because of that, its growth could be deferred for some years or even a decade. Such a correction could also turn into a crisis. But in that case, the region, as well as the world, is likely to come to China's aid, given that East Asian countries have become deeply integrated with China's economy. In short, unless there is a complete collapse of the country—which is at this juncture a remote possibility—China is bound to become a major economic entity, although in per capita terms it will not be able to catch up with the United States until the middle of the century.

The Chinese people and the Chinese leadership have been upbeat about their achievements, and they are making use of them cleverly. However, they have to admit that the problems they are facing due to high growth and to the profound changes occurring in their society are also huge and complicated. These problems have indeed become their main concern. They include unemployment, income inequality between the coastal and inland regions, corruption and governance issues, state banks' nonperforming loans, inefficient state enterprises, the plight of the farmers, and last but not least, the challenges of political development.

The principal internal constraints on China's growth are institutional, namely the lack of the rule of law, uncertainty regarding property rights, the inefficiency of state enterprises, and the profound weakness of the financial system and intellectual property rights. Important symptoms of these weaknesses have been the reliance on foreign entrepreneurship and offshore financial and legal centers, particularly Hong Kong. Behind these weaknesses is something more profound, namely a political system that may not be suitable for an increasingly sophisticated economy and society. The political transition from a one-party state to a more democratic regime is problematic and difficult, as shown by Mexico's experience.

China has to confront not only domestic challenges but also external ones. China's extraordinary success in export markets has been a powerful engine for its growth. But it is questionable whether this can continue now that China has become such a huge player in world trade and given that its economy is already so open.

The challenges ahead for China are large by any standard. But it is a good bet that China will continue to grow rapidly for at least another two to three decades. This will require continuing and painful reforms. But the alternative—i.e., a slowing down of the country's economic dynamism—is not an attractive option for China's policymakers.

The Chinese leadership understands these domestic challenges, and they have tried very hard to overcome them. Especially with regard to the political development challenge, they are trying out schemes to give political space to the lowest level (i.e., villages) to elect representatives from among more than one candidate—and from among candidates who are not all from the Chinese Communist Party. But these steps are considered by many to be too slow and too timid.

The critical issue and challenge for China's leadership will arise when its economic growth and development need correction (e.g., a drop in the growth rate to very low levels, such as below 5 percent). At that point, the question will be whether they are willing to take the necessary measures and whether they are able to do so within the limits of the political system. A key question will be whether unity among the leadership can be preserved to support such corrective actions.

India, too, is suffering from many constraints. Low savings in the public sector impose a significant limitation on capital formation. The country's political and legal systems, though well developed, are cumbersome and inefficient. Its political agenda lacks a focus on development. In addition, the growing supply of labor has not been matched by a rise in demand. As a result, overall employment has risen by only 1 percent per year over the past decade or so. Literacy remains low. For faster growth to be achieved, there is a need for substantially higher savings and investment, greater inflows of FDI, and much more rapid industrialization.

India's relationship with East Asia has just started to deepen in the last several years as it has adopted its "Look East" policy, spurred both by an attraction to East Asia's economic growth and by a desire to escape the constraints of South Asia. However, since India's economy has not really opened up yet due to political constraints, and since it is following a model of development that differs from the East Asian model, its involvement in the region will take more time to materialize. It will come, but further changes in India's domestic economy and regulations (and perhaps in its domestic politics as well) are the *sine qua non* of India's increasing involvement with East Asia. It may take another five to ten years for that to happen more profoundly.

India is now already involved in the East Asia Summit, and its greater engagement with the region could be useful. The summit, as a body dealing with strategic issues, should indeed be the right forum for India, since the latter has left its footprint in the region historically and since more will be expected of its participation in East Asia in the future.

The Shifting Balance of Power

If East Asia continues to grow with Japan, China, and India driving its development, it will indeed become the most important region of the globe and the balance of power will certainly shift. That shift could occur sometime in the mid-21st century, beginning first in the economic sphere, then in the political field, and possibly also in the security field.

The end of the 19th century and the beginning of the 20th century showed that economic growth and dynamism alone were not adequate to create peace and stability in Europe and around the world when inadequate attention was paid to the politico-security field. The result was World War I, followed by the emergence of extremism such as Nazism and communism, World War II, and the Cold War, which ended in the waning days of the 20th century.

The relationship between a rising superpower and an established one, such as that between China and the United States, is never an easy one. However, it does not necessarily result in confrontation, as shown by the relationship between Great Britain, the superpower of the 19th century, and the United States, its 20th-century successor. An important recent development has been the establishment of certain principles in the relations between the United States and China that originated with the suggestion by then Deputy Secretary of State Robert Zoellick to recognize Chinese stakeholdership in the global and international order and in its institutions. This is now being promoted by Treasury Secretary Hank Paulson. And while still in its early stages, this new approach has started to work, especially on the North Korean nuclear proliferation issue. This principle will work if China takes its responsibilities seriously and if the United States accepts some temporary exceptions that can be agreed upon through dialogue.

Today, the economies of the world have again become interdependent and more integrated. But the political relations must also be handled correctly in order to maintain the peace and stability needed to ensure the sustainability of the world's economic growth and dynamism. International institutions and norms were established after World War II to maintain stable political relationships, but they need adjustment and reform.

The international system itself was placed in danger by the terrorist attack on the United States on September 11, 2001. It appeared as if there was going to be a clash of civilizations à la Samuel Huntington's treatise. Moreover, there was a danger that the United States, which was in a state of shock for a few years following the attack, would act as a "unilateralist" superpower and would go it alone. But balance, sensibility, and nuance appear to have been restored by the midterm US Congressional elections, held in November 2006.

Regional institutions in East Asia will also contribute to restoring balance in the global and regional order. They are becoming more important institutions as they have deepened their cooperation within a limited region and are able to achieve more in every field of activity.

In order for this shift in the balance of power to take place peacefully in East Asia, two basic things have to happen. First, the shift must occur gradually and should not be considered a zero-sum game by the established powers, mainly the United States and the European Union (EU). They will continue to have an important role in global governance because East Asia alone cannot maintain global order and institutions. In the end, there needs to be a concert of major powers to lead and influence the world.

Second, the new emerging powers, meaning those in East Asia, should also prepare themselves well. That means not only sharing stakeholdership but also responsibility. They have to prepare and adjust their own value systems to be compatible with what have become global values, namely the rule of law, good governance, democracy, human rights, and social justice. They should accept that democracy and social justice are values and principles that are valid not only nationally, but also globally. Implementation may be influenced by history, stages of development, and values, but the basic criteria should be the same for every country and society.

The change is not going to be easy, and that is why it should be done step by step and with patience on the part of East Asia. This process has already begun with the reallocation of votes in the International Monetary Fund toward new emerging economies—China, Korea, Turkey, and Mexico—to the detriment of some EU members. It was demonstrated that even this simple "transfer" could be difficult. More difficulties have been and will be faced with efforts to adjust and reform the UN system in accordance with the new strategic changes occurring globally.

THE STEPS AHEAD FOR REGIONAL COMMUNITY BUILDING

East Asia has an obligation to do its part in global governance. One of the objectives of an integrated East Asia is to be able to contribute to the global system, so as not to be accused of "free riding," benefiting from and using the global system for national or regional interests only. On the other hand, the established powers, mainly the "West" (i.e., the United States and the EU), should also be willing to share the responsibility for global governance and allow the "new forces," mainly the emerging markets in East Asia, to learn and to prepare themselves for assuming more of that role. China, for instance, needs to understand that its relations with rogue states such as Iran, Sudan, and Myanmar will be viewed in light of its international obligations and its new role. However, some exceptions could be allowed. After all, China was not present at the creation of the global order and institutions after World War II, and although it is now willing to accept them wholly, it will need time to adjust. As the "new kid on the block," China is still learning, but it is generally willing to follow the accepted rules.

The main challenge for East Asia is to know what should be done in the short term and what can be done in the longer term. This will depend on how quickly East Asian regionalism progresses and the regional community can be established.

Challenges abound to the realization of the idea of an East Asia community. First, it should not be measured against the EU, which is rules based and driven by strong institutions. As countries in the East Asian region are so diverse, the East Asia community needs to get its members to trust each other through strengthened relations and cooperation. This will take time and can only be achieved through a gradual, long-term approach.

The first phase of cooperation should be in the economic field, because market forces have made the integration of the economies in the region a reality. Trade among East Asian economies now represents 55 percent of the region's total trade, which is almost equal to intra-EU trade (65 percent) and already higher than intra-NAFTA trade (45 percent). Also, inflows of investment into the region have been huge—not only into China, but also returning to ASEAN. In 2006, FDI into ASEAN amounted to US$52.3 billion, while China's FDI inflows (not including the financial sector) were US$63 billion.

However, the next phase of integration needs proactive government involvement, because politics inevitably start to affect economic co-operation and could derail the entire process. This is precisely what happened in Europe from the mid-19th century to the mid-20th century, culminating in World War I and World War II, because Europe did not get the politics right, especially in dealing with a rising Germany. That resulted in stagnant trade and economic relations, and Europe experienced constant conflict for almost one century prior to the establishment of the EU. It was the new regional order and institutions that helped to stabilize Europe during the Cold War, in addition to the presence of the United States through NATO.

Some progress has already been made in East Asia in terms of concrete cooperative measures through the Chiang Mai Initiative to help prevent a recurrence of the type of financial crisis that struck in 1997–1998. Similarly, there have been attempts to solidify economic cooperation through free trade agreements (FTAs) between ASEAN and China, ASEAN and Japan, and ASEAN and South Korea, which hopefully will lead to an FTA that covers all of East Asia. However, there are many obstacles to realizing the goal of deeper regional cooperation.

One obstacle is the China-Japan relationship, which has been hampered by history, nationalism, competition for leadership in the region, and competing claims in the East China Sea. Prime Minister Abe's visit to China in October 2006 marked a new beginning, and hopefully relations will continue to improve. Economic relations between the two are doing well, and people-to-people relations continue to intensify, especially among the younger people. Prime Minister Abe undertook a new initiative to increase youth exchange. And a binational committee of historians was established in late 2006, tasked with studying recent history and presenting its research findings within two years. In addition, the two countries agreed to hold exchanges of leaders on a more regular basis. This began with Foreign Minister Li Zhaoxing's Tokyo visit in February 2007 and Prime Minister Wen Jiabao's visit in April 2007, while plans have been made for deepened military cooperation through visits and dialogues.

Another obstacle is the US relationship with the East Asia community. The United States has always played an important role in East Asia in terms of economics, politics, and security. Therefore, a modality must be found to involve it in the East Asia community. At the same time, there is also the recognition that East Asia, which has been so integrated economically and to a certain extent also politically, needs to have a kind of a Group of Eight (G-8) or a concert of powers that can discuss and make decisions on the strategic issues of the region with the aim of maintaining peace, stability, and development in the region. For this reason the United States should be invited to the East Asia Summit, and in so doing, the East Asia Summit will be upgraded into a concert of powers for East Asia, a kind of a G-8 for East Asia. It should become the forum for strategic issues: economic, political, and security matters. How ASEAN should be represented in this forum should be decided by ASEAN itself, with the consent of other members. It could be represented by the newly accepted idea of having an ASEAN "troika" of the past, present, and next chairmen of ASEAN, or it could be represented by the current chairman and secretary-general of ASEAN. The condition that members should sign the Treaty of Amity and Cooperation has been the reason for the US reluctance to become involved. However, this should not pose a real hindrance for the United States because while this is a treaty in form, its content is more political than legal.

The East Asia Summit could take place either biannually, alternating with the APEC Summit, or it could be organized annually and be held back-to-back with the APEC Summit. APEC, as the main mechanism promoting increased cooperation between the western and the eastern parts of the Pacific should be maintained as an important regional institution to keep the idea of Pacific cooperation intact. To gain back the relevance that it has lost, however, APEC should maintain its core focus—i.e., economic cooperation—while placing greater stress on domestic structural issues, or "behind-the-border" issues, rather than only emphasizing trade.

There is also the consideration of including Russia and the EU at a later stage. Russia's economic interests and interactions, including in the energy field, are mainly with the EU. The latter, for its part, already has a structure for engaging with East Asia in the form of the Asia-Europe Meeting. With more economic interaction in the medium term, Russia's membership could be entertained in the future. On the other hand, the EU's preoccupation with its own region will postpone its membership in the East Asia Summit for the time being.

ASEAN+3 should be the main institution for economic and functional cooperation in the region. In the implementation of its work program, it should be pragmatic and open to involving others that are relevant to the program on a case-by-case basis. For instance, all members of the

East Asia Summit could be included in responses to pandemic diseases, and Australia could be invited to participate in discussions of monetary and financial affairs.

In the security field, the ASEAN Regional Forum (ARF) could be the vehicle for the implementation of confidence-building measures and initiatives on human security or nontraditional security matters, including pandemic diseases and global terrorism. Meanwhile, the Six-Party Talks, if successful in addressing the nuclear proliferation of North Korea, could be transformed into a mechanism to more broadly promote security cooperation on traditional "hard" security matters for East Asia. For that to happen, it also should have ASEAN's participation.

Another constraint, however, is ASEAN's position in the "driver's seat" of regional community building in East Asia. Many questions have been raised as to whether ASEAN could really lead the East Asian regional institutions, such as ASEAN+3 and the East Asia Summit, despite representing only 10 percent of the entire East Asian economy. However, ASEAN has been put in the driver's seat because the two natural leaders, China and Japan, cannot assume that role at this juncture. It is clear that ASEAN still needs to strengthen its capacity to be able to actually drive the community-building process. In order to give greater weight to ASEAN so it can more effectively play this role, ASEAN's capabilities should be upgraded and South Korea might support ASEAN in carrying out the duties of the "driver." Also, ASEAN must implement the various measures toward realizing the ASEAN Community that were outlined in 2003 in the Bali Concord II.

At this stage, the leadership role of ASEAN consists mainly of organizing the meetings and chairing them, but in practice ASEAN has allowed the "Plus Three" countries (China, Japan, and South Korea) to come up with initiatives and proposals to be discussed, decided on, and implemented. In other instances, working groups are being cochaired by ASEAN members and the Plus Three members. For the time being, this arrangement seems to be working, and it should be continued for the near future.

CONTRIBUTIONS TO GLOBAL GOVERNANCE

Despite the various constraints and limitations, in the near future East Asia should, through regional institutions such as ASEAN+3 and the East Asia Summit, strive to support important global norms and institutions. It has been obvious that East Asia should and would like to participate in supporting the global order, its rules, obligations, and institutions. It has only just started to do so, and more needs to be done.

First, in terms of nonproliferation, East Asia has a real problem with North Korea. The Six-Party Talks have been the focus of regional efforts in Northeast Asia, and the greater East Asian institutions such as ASEAN+3, the ARF, and the East Asia Summit have strongly supported these efforts, especially in giving political support to the Six-Party Talks and implementing the sanctions as laid down by the UN Security Council.

Second, in order to help maintain an open global trading system, East Asian countries should strive for a successful conclusion of the World Trade Organization Doha Development Round. At the November 2006 APEC Economic Leaders' Meeting in Hanoi, APEC members reiterated their commitment to do so, and East Asia should also push very hard for this. The chances are slim, but given their dependence on open trade, it is important for East Asian countries that these efforts be continued until every avenue has been exhausted.

A reliance on bilateral and regional FTAs alone will not be sufficient because the trade distortions, diversions, and discrimination they create can only be overcome by multilateral agreements. Time is running out and the fate of free trade for the next five years is in the balance because the US administration's ability to negotiate on trade issues is severely limited with a Democratic majority in Congress.

Third, there needs to be greater support and cooperation on matters of the global public good such as climate change, which has already shown its ugly face in East Asia. Some East Asian countries that have been experiencing fantastic economic growth have also joined the ranks of the largest global polluters. Serious contributions from East Asia, the fastest developing part of the globe, have become a real necessity. The Cebu Declaration on East Asian Energy Security that was adopted at the second East Asia Summit was a good start. The implementation of its worthy principles is another matter, and ASEAN should push for this, starting with policies to promote more efficient energy use, with Japan serving as a model. It is also clear that an early US commitment to these same efforts would hasten East Asia's readiness to support such initiatives.

Fourth, in tandem with environmental issues, there is the problem of energy security and resource availability. Some real efforts and studies are needed so that East Asia can overcome its problems, contribute to a more efficient global market, and prevent the outbreak of conflict over energy and other natural resources. The urgency of this issue was also recognized in the Cebu Declaration. If East Asia is serious about environmental issues and about the impact of natural resource limits on its economic development, then it really should come up with a new model of economic development that recognizes these limits to growth.

Fifth, as we have discovered with severe acute respiratory syndrome, or SARS, efforts on pandemic diseases are important in terms of human security, not only in our region but also globally. Diseases such as the avian influenza have become a major challenge for the region. Again, there is agreement on the policies that the region should pursue together, but implementation and coordination remain serious problems.

Sixth, there are many other human security and nontraditional security issues that are also important to look at, including international crimes such as human trafficking, money laundering, and drug trafficking. Nontraditional security issues are as important for the region as traditional "hard" security issues. And the region is more willing to cooperate on these issues. This provides an opening for the ARF to become active and do something. It cannot stay forever as a "talk shop" if it wants to remain relevant to the future of East Asia.

Seventh, in relation to the sixth point, there is the threat of global and regional terrorism. This challenge necessitates regional and global cooperation, including from East Asia. This will be a long-term effort, and it goes hand-in-hand with measures to promote sustainable development and good governance. In terms of Islamic extremism, "moderate" Muslims should be able to overcome the harmful influences of the radicals on the Muslim community if they can show their community that "democracy" with "social justice" can work in their societies and states so that there is no more need for the establishment of a theocratic Muslim state.

Eighth, the reforms of the UN, however complicated and difficult, should be supported because the UN system is the only global institution we have. The UN has not always been effective, but it is for that precise reason that efforts should be made to improve and reform it. Having benefited from the UN system to a large extent, East Asian countries and regional institutions should give it greater support.

Other cases concerning global norms and institutions relate to problems of sovereignty and domestic issues and must be dealt with by national governments. East Asian regional institutions are not ready at this stage to represent national governments. This could happen only if integration becomes much deeper and nations agree to surrender part of their national sovereignty on specific issues. On the economic side, they are willing to do so, such as on the Chiang Mai Initiative and FTAs or on the need for a dispute settlement mechanism in trade and investment.

In the longer term, if East Asia becomes more integrated, some co-operation on developing global norms and institutions could happen. East Asia has to prepare itself for this future task. In practical terms, those participating in East Asian regional cooperation must also become active in the development of global norms and institutions.

Until recently, of all the East Asian countries, only Japan had done its part on these global issues. In the last few years, China has started to be active as well and has taken some responsibility as a permanent member of the UN Security Council. South Korea has also done well in the last few years. Other countries have been participating in UN peacekeeping operations and in other activities, but this is still rather limited. More can and should be done by the East Asian countries individually and as a regional grouping in the near future.

CONCLUSION

In conclusion, it can be said that on issues related to humanitarian matters or human security—especially as manifested in various non-traditional security issues such as the environment, migration, human trafficking, drug trafficking, money laundering, pandemic disease, and global or regional terrorism—where politics is in the background, co-operation in East Asia can be established and implemented quite readily. On the other hand, if sovereignty issues or intervention in domestic affairs are involved, then a lot of work is needed.

It remains to be seen how quickly this might happen following some real changes, such as in the case of the ASEAN Charter in East Asian regionalism. It could and has happened initially in the economic sphere and subsequently at the political and security level, but efforts to get it done are critically important.

It is also important that East Asian regional institution building should not only come from above, meaning from the governments, but that equal weight should be given to people-to-people efforts and cooperation. Without their support, as ASEAN has found out, cooperation will not come quickly or deeply. In ASEAN, the ASEAN People's Assembly is partly fulfilling the role of civil society representation.

ASEAN has been the model of East Asian regional institution building because the history and diversity of the region have been factors in defining regional cooperation efforts. Cooperation, therefore, has been built on human relations and economic cooperation. In the case of East Asia, it has mainly been the businessmen who took the initiative and promoted regional economic cooperation, primarily through trade. From the outset, it has been a process from below, and the government's role is only now becoming important because, after a certain intensity of cooperation has been reached, there is a need for rules and institutions, and this is where governments come in.

Concerning global responsibilities, East Asia has started to fulfill its role, especially Japan, which is an older player on the international scene. India has always been strong in peacekeeping and other global matters pertaining to disarmament and nonproliferation (although now its credibility has been dented due to its nuclear weapons acquisition and testing). Even China has started to play its role as a responsible stakeholder, and has curtailed its mercantilist policies to a certain extent, such as in the cases of Darfur, Myanmar (with ASEAN), and even Iran (at the UN Security Council). Also, China has been very active in peacekeeping and in regional institution building, and has pursued very active and responsible policies at the regional level. But, of course, it could and should do more in the future. ASEAN also has been active at the UN level (e.g., in nonproliferation efforts and peacekeeping) and at the regional level.

There are good prospects then, for East Asia to do as well as can be expected concerning global responsibilities in most cases. Of course, further work is still needed, particularly where most members are newcomers to the role.

For ASEAN, the creation of an ASEAN Charter has become a must, because cooperation is not only advancing in the areas of trade and economic cooperation alone but also in the political and even in the security fields and among its people. This is a natural outgrowth of the increased intense cooperation and is also necessary to be able to respond to the new strategic challenges in the region.

The idea of an ASEAN Charter was preceded by the Bali Concord II, which prepared for an ASEAN Community to be established based on three poles of cooperation: economic, security, and sociocultural.

The idea of a community will be strengthened by having a charter that spells out the principles, objectives, institutions, and processes of decision making. The idea is to make ASEAN a more rules- and institution-based entity that will be able to cope with new fields of cooperation and deeper cooperation.

This will also gradually be done in the context of building an East Asia community. Where increasing cooperation requires such rules and institutions, they should be established in the future. For the medium term, East Asian regional institutions such as ASEAN+3 and the East Asia Summit should also have common principles on which to base cooperation, namely rules and institutions to organize them more permanently and the necessary transparency in decision making.

Even China has recognized the need for, and shown its willingness to include, principles such as democracy, human rights, the rule of law, and good governance, because they are the common heritage of mankind. Of course, the differing histories, cultural values, and stages of development among states in the region have some influence on the implementation of these common principles and rules, and therefore it is wisest to take a step-by-step approach in introducing them while working consistently to expand their scope.

In comparison with ASEAN, which is much readier for deeper integration despite remaining a grouping of sovereign states, East Asian regionalism will be more firmly based on nation-states. That is why while the "ASEAN Community" can have a capital "C" at the front of the word "Community," the "East Asia community" should, at least temporarily, be written with a small "c." While the EU is more strongly based on common principles, ideologies, and views (due to its common history), the East Asia community will be less so, at least for some time to come. But things are going to develop—and develop fast—in East Asia, and the outcome could always be a surprise.

3

Obstacles to East Asia Community Building

Carolina G. Hernandez

Much has been accomplished since East Asia community building began shortly after the Asian financial crisis of 1997. Through the initiative of South Korean President Kim Dae-jung, the East Asia Vision Group (EAVG) was formed. Consisting of nongovernmental experts from the ten ASEAN member countries and China, Japan, and South Korea (ASEAN+3), it was tasked with developing concrete proposals for East Asia cooperation. The EAVG submitted its report in 2001, after which ASEAN+3 appointed an East Asia Study Group (EASG), consisting of representatives of the ASEAN+3 governments. The EASG submitted its report in 2002, recommending several short-term and long-term measures to build an East Asia community. Among its recommendations was that the ASEAN+3 Summit should evolve into an East Asia Summit. This process was seen as a slow and evolutionary process and limited to the geographical confines of the ASEAN+3 countries.

In the meantime, cooperation in economic, financial, and functional areas has been promoted among the ASEAN+3 countries, although in the form of bilateral agreements and "coalition of the willing" arrangements. Aware of the significant implications of broader security issues in their program of regional cooperation, they have also added items in the security field to their agenda, including maritime security and counterterrorism, and they have expanded their economic and functional agenda to include gender issues and poverty alleviation.

In building a regional community, East Asia subscribes to the concept of "open regionalism," which means that, in spite of their goal of promoting closer and enhanced cooperation across various dimensions among the ASEAN+3 countries, it does not intend to become a bloc that excludes other relevant players, particularly in the economic, functional, and even political dimensions.

However, in addition to the structural and historical difficulties facing East Asia community building, there are a number of obstacles, some existent and some potential, that could undermine the process. These include a gamut of issues that span this region of immense diversity, a group of states faced with many divides that could be obstacles to East Asia community building. Among them are a wide range of political systems; different levels of economic development; and disparities in human development, including disparities in income inequality and poverty.

The experience of the most successful regional integration scheme, that of the European Union (EU), shows that community building is facilitated by a relatively low level of sharp differences in the political and socioeconomic characteristics of the members of a proposed community. It is conventional wisdom to claim that the EU countries are more homogeneous than other regions in the world, but the EU countries themselves are quick to deny this claim. They point to their belief that, although they might come from the so-called Greco-Roman-Christian civilization, there are in fact many distinctions among them, borne of their distinct geographical circumstances and historical evolution, and that these would need to be diluted for them to become a genuine community with a common identity. Consequently, the EU established a set of criteria for membership, including the provision of "cohesion funds" for political and economic reforms to erode the differences between the old members and candidate members. Only after the implementation of these reforms can candidate members earn full admission into the community.

Further testimony to the importance of a set of common socioeconomic and political characteristics in realizing a community can be found in the recent change of heart among ASEAN leaders—the same ASEAN leaders who excessively celebrated the diversity of its members in the past. In recent years, they have come to recognize that a narrowing of the ASEAN economic divide is needed for deeper integration into an ASEAN Economic Community; that the achievement of an ASEAN Security Community depends on the shaping and sharing of norms and political development that would promote greater participation, rule of law, justice, and democracy among the member states; and that the building of a community of caring and sharing societies (the ASEAN Socio-Cultural Community) is a necessary component of building an ASEAN community. Thus, community building in East Asia requires the erosion of wide disparities among prospective members. Conversely, the continued existence of these wide disparities could serve as real and potential obstacles to community building.

This chapter identifies and analyzes structural, historical, political, and socioeconomic obstacles to East Asia community building from a Southeast Asian perspective. The structural dimension deals with the presence of two great regional powers, China and Japan, with the potential for future rivalry in a region of small and medium-sized states. The historical dimension relates to past acts of aggression and colonization by Japan against China, Korea, and most Southeast Asian states, a historical legacy that remains a factor in the continuing trust and confidence deficit among states in the region, particularly in Northeast Asia.

The political and socioeconomic obstacles highlight the case of ASEAN, which is acknowledged as occupying the "driver's seat" in the East Asia community-building project, at least for the time being. Among the key obstacles to be addressed in the political dimension are the absence of regional leadership at both the ASEAN and East Asia levels; the diversity of political systems, governing norms, and values; the lack of common perspectives and policies on foreign relations and security; the domestic political challenges preoccupying regional states, including their unfinished nation- and state-building processes; the failure to embed community building in the core national interest of ASEAN countries; and an overall aversion to institutions.

The key socioeconomic obstacles that hinder East Asia community building include the unfinished economic reforms in many countries and uncoordinated free trade agreements (FTAs); persistent competitive elements in regional economies; wide differences in levels of economic development; as well as varying levels of human development, including large income disparities and widespread poverty, particularly within and across Southeast Asian countries. The discussion of this set of obstacles will highlight the varying levels of human development because other chapters in this volume cover the economic dimension of community building in the region.

STRUCTURAL AND HISTORICAL OBSTACLES

Despite a number of promising recent developments in Sino-Japanese relations—increasing economic interdependence, political cooperation through the Six-Party Talks process in dealing with the nuclear weapons development program adopted by North Korea, and enhanced cooperation in several functional areas (in particular, environmental protection)—the fact that the structure of power in East Asia is dominated by these two potential rivals hinders community building in the region. The survival of historical animosities, as expressed in the occasional eruption of tensions in relation to visits to the Yasukuni Shrine by Japanese leaders such as Junichiro Koizumi and Shinzo Abe and in anti-Japanese public demonstrations in China, combines with the tenacity of territorial disputes to inhibit a genuine reconciliation between these two powers.

In addition, despite protestations to the contrary, the concern that there could be a future rivalry for regional leadership between these two nations has not subsided. Japan's military alliance with the United States, its perceived partiality toward Taiwan in cross-strait relations, its increasing participation in international peacekeeping, and its pursuit of a permanent seat on the UN Security Council, combined with suspicions about Japanese remilitarization as Tokyo begins to transform its international role by seeking the status of a "normal state," do not help to quell China's concerns. Nor do recent moves to try to amend the peace constitution and to change the name of Japan's Self-Defense Forces, which are seen as further evidence of Japanese "remilitarization."

To be fair, these developments are only the natural consequence of new realities emerging both inside Japan and in the external environment. These concerns are rooted in the structural rivalry between East Asia's major powers but are most likely unfounded given Japan's sustained policy of peaceful relations with its neighbors; its realization that its policy toward the region during the interwar period and World War II was counterproductive; and its strong alliance with the United States, which should obviate the emergence of a remilitarized Japan.

On the other hand, China's economic rise and its perceived future re-placement of Japan as East Asia's economic powerhouse; Beijing's gains in its diplomacy vis-à-vis ASEAN; its proactive search for both diplomatic influence worldwide and energy resources in Africa, Central Asia, and Latin America; its creation of a China-centered regional cooperation scheme that excludes both Japan and the United States (i.e., the Shanghai Cooperation Organization); and its refusal to have Japan become a permanent member of the UN Security Council reinforce suspicion of its bid to rival Japan in the future. There is also the concern that, although economic interdependence and integration are leading the process of regional community building and China is committed to its peaceful development, political and security considerations would likely prevail in the event that China's core national interests were to run counter to its economic goals. Related to this is the view that contemporary Chinese nationalism is based to a large extent on perceived historical wrongs against China by external powers, cross-strait relations, and the preservation of China's territorial integrity. These bases are likely to survive in the event that the present regime in Beijing fails to meet the people's material expectations.

South Korea joins the ASEAN states in being caught up in this great power rivalry. Keeping China and Japan within the context of an East Asia community is a good way of moderating the likelihood of com-petition, which would be inimical to the interests of all states in the region. South Korea is also an important actor in Northeast Asian reconciliation—a process about which ASEAN nations have some les-sons to share, having reconciled not only amongst themselves, but also with Japan since the 1970s.

If these structural and historical difficulties remain unresolved, the proj-ect of realizing an East Asia community will be in serious doubt. Small and medium-sized states in ASEAN might find themselves torn between these two powers. ASEAN is already sought after by Beijing and Tokyo in their bid to outdo each other in economic partnership with ASEAN. Japan is seen as trying to keep up with a fast-moving and responsive China, as seen in the building of the China-ASEAN Free Trade Area. Although China has not caught up with Japan as a development partner of ASEAN, trade relations between China and ASEAN countries are on the rise. Japan continues to lead in providing official development assistance (ODA) to ASEAN coun-tries (39 percent of ASEAN's total ODA), as well as to China. Although there has been an increase in ASEAN-China trade relations in recent years, Japan's trade with ASEAN (13.7 percent of ASEAN's total trade) remains larger than ASEAN-China trade (8.5 percent), while Japan's foreign direct investment (FDI) based on the balance of payments to ASEAN countries constitutes 11.6 percent of ASEAN's total inward FDI.[1]

POLITICAL OBSTACLES

Among the political obstacles to East Asia community building is the leadership of the project. This obstacle operates at two levels: the intra-ASEAN level and the East Asia level. At the intra-ASEAN level, the loss of Indonesia as ASEAN's informal leader—a consequence of that country's domestic political and economic instability brought about by the 1997 financial crisis—hinders community building in the sense that consensus among the ASEAN member states is harder to achieve, while measures to move and act together are slower to develop. It must be recalled that Indonesia enabled the holding of the third ASEAN Summit in the Philippines in 1987, even as other members hesitated to come to Manila due to security concerns following a serious coup attempt against the Aquino government. Former Malaysian Prime Minister Mahathir Mohamad also refused to come to Manila until the Philippines dropped its territorial claim to Sabah. Through former President Suharto's exertion of influence-cum-pressure, the third summit was held successfully, as Indonesia—with Philippine consent—sent a naval ship that docked in Manila Bay to provide security to the leaders during the summit. Moreover, despite its serious misgivings about wider regional economic cooperation, Malaysia came on board the APEC forum after Indonesia's persistent persuasion. It is notable that such a leading performance among ASEAN member states in the context of APEC has not been seen since the 1997 financial crisis threw Indonesia into turmoil.

For the time being, ASEAN is in the driver's seat of East Asia community building because not one of the "Plus Three" countries (China, Japan, and South Korea) would be prepared to see either of the other two perform this role. However, ASEAN's bid to serve as the driving force or the core of East Asia community building could be undermined without some form of leadership, such as the role played by Indonesia prior to 1997. Of late, some other ASEAN member states have sought to

---

1. Data on ODA, trade, and FDI are for 2004 and are from the International Monetary Fund (IMF), *Direction of Trade Statistics Yearbook 2005* (Washington DC: IMF, 2005) and *Balance of Payments Statistics Yearbook 2005* (Washington DC: IMF, 2005).

fill this role, such as Thailand during the Democrat Party and Thaksin eras, Singapore in the ASEAN Economic Community project, Malaysia in the Non-aligned Movement, the Philippines in the ASEAN Socio-Cultural Community project, and Indonesia once again in the ASEAN Security Community project. Yet these are no substitutes for a leader for all issues and for all seasons, as existed in the pre-1997 days. Singapore has shown a willingness to succeed Indonesia in playing that type of leading role in ASEAN. However, in spite of its numerous advantages, taking the leadership role in ASEAN would not come easy for this wealthy and efficient city-state amidst such larger states as Indonesia, Malaysia, and Thailand.

If ASEAN is handicapped by the lack of a leader, its bid to stay in the driver's seat in East Asia community building will be at risk. At this level, while ASEAN is regarded as the driving force in East Asia community building for now, the question of whether it can continue to be such a force in the foreseeable future worries its ten member states. ASEAN's combined economic output is lower than that of any of the Plus Three countries. The economic output of the ASEAN 10 stands roughly at US\$1 billion, compared with Japan's US\$4.4 trillion, China's US\$2.6 trillion, and South Korea's US\$900 billion.[2] ASEAN's economic growth before the 1997 financial crisis had been stimulated by close aid, trade, and investment ties with Japan, while its economic recovery since the crisis has to a large extent been spurred by its trade ties with China.

Thus, the drive to maintain ASEAN's centrality in the East Asia community was an overriding concern during the tenure of Lao PDR as chair of the ASEAN Standing Committee in 2004, during which all ten ASEAN states put their heads together to ensure that ASEAN remained at the center of this regional project. Many within ASEAN circles argue that it is in the interest of the Plus Three countries to buoy ASEAN's bid to remain in the driver's seat by providing assistance and support in narrowing the development gaps within ASEAN through various programs—including human resource, institutional, information, and infrastructure development—in addition to enhancing their trade and investment relations with ASEAN.

If ASEAN cannot be the driving force of community building in East Asia, neither can China, Japan, or South Korea. As already noted, any bid

---

2. These figures are based on 2006 GDP data from the IMF's April 2007 World Economic Outlook data, available at www.imf.org/external/pubs/ft/weo/2007/01/data/index.aspx.

for leadership by either China or Japan would not earn the support of the other. Nor would South Korea earn the support of either China or Japan. So for now, ASEAN is the driving force by default. But to what extent can this be sustained?

Moreover, in spite of Kim Dae-jung's leadership in the EAVG and the EASG, the region does not have the equivalent of a Monnet or a Schuman, who so successfully advocated the creation of a European community. With the passing of President Kim Dae-jung from the political scene, South Korea was not able to sustain the initiative for an East Asia community. The East Asia Summit envisioned by the EASG to evolve from the ASEAN+3 Summit was hijacked by ASEAN and has now presented another challenge to community building in the form of an enlarged and no longer geographic East Asia concept that extends beyond ASEAN+3.

Another political obstacle is the existence of diverse political systems, governing norms, and values, not just in the broader East Asia but even within the 40-year-old ASEAN. The political diversity among ASEAN countries has created problems at the bilateral and regional levels. Treatment of the nationals of one country by another due to differences in governing norms has resulted in tension on occasions, or in refugees spilling into the territory of neighboring states. At the same time, the outside world continues to expect ASEAN to be accountable for the failings of Myanmar's military junta, thereby creating a degree of discomfort, if not embarrassment, for the grouping. Its political dialogue with the EU was suspended temporarily on account of Myanmar's admission into ASEAN in 1997. Attempts are now being made to narrow this diversity through the ASEAN Security Community, and particularly through the shaping and sharing of norms and political development toward a just, democratic, and more participative ASEAN that also observes human rights and the rule of law. The Plus Three countries also have different political systems, with China still being a regime run by the Communist Party, while Japan and South Korea are democracies.

Thus, in East Asia, one finds a wide range of political systems: a military junta, a feudal kingdom, three Communist Party–run states, a reversed democracy, an illiberal democracy, two constrained democracies, two unconsolidated democracies, and two consolidated democracies. Despite increasing economic integration, their common norms and values remain highly Westphalian—hardly conducive to community building. The latter requires common institutions of governance to become effective and meaningful to its constituencies, a requirement seen as opposed to the core values of the Westphalian state.

Within ASEAN alone, what is apparent is the prevalence of national egoism rather than regionalism among member states, and a failure to make regionalism part of each country's core national interests. This debilitating situation can hopefully be corrected with a progressive and people-oriented ASEAN Charter that would establish ASEAN as a legal entity and intergovernmental organization; rationalize and adopt new institutions for more effective governance; empower its secretary-general with new authority, especially to monitor the implementation of agreements; make compliance no longer voluntary; institutionalize consultation with nongovernmental constituencies such as parliamentarians, business, academe, and civil society organizations; establish dispute settlement mechanisms not only for economic and trade disputes but also for political, territorial, and other types of disputes; and institute other institutional innovations.

Unfortunately, the ASEAN Charter approved at the Leaders' Summit in November 2007, beyond making ASEAN an international legal entity, merely codified its existing processes whereby consensus decision making and voluntary implementation of agreements remain central. New structures in the secretariat and new responsibilities given to the secretary-general were not matched by resources. Nonetheless, the charter contained principles and norms to propagate human rights, the rule of law, and democracy, regardless of the fact that its enabling provision for the establishment of a regional human rights body was vague.

Another political obstacle is the absence of common perspectives and policies on foreign affairs and security. In particular, differences in ideology and relations with the superpowers of the Cold War days, as well as historical and geostrategic factors, help explain this situation. The US-led military alliance network in East Asia includes Japan, South Korea, the Philippines, and Thailand, while Singapore is pro–United States in its overall defense policy despite the absence of formal bilateral ties. Looking at the Proliferation Security Initiative to counter terrorism, for example, the first East Asian countries to join the United States were Japan and Singapore, followed in 2006 by the Philippines and Thailand, the latter two as major non-NATO allies of the United States. There are varying types of relations with the United States among the rest of the nations of East Asia, with China, Lao PDR, Malaysia, and Myanmar being among the more critical of US policy in general. As a result, it will take a while for ASEAN to develop common foreign affairs and security perspectives or policies and even longer for the Plus Three countries, given the more serious structural and historical problems that continue to exist among them.

In addition, domestic political challenges also pose obstacles to East Asia community building as states place priority on addressing these domestic concerns first. The challenges include regime survival, regime legitimacy, and the incomplete processes of nation and state building in Southeast Asia. These are issues that continue to preoccupy countries in ASEAN, taking efforts and resources away from the earnest pursuit of community building. Moreover, a related issue is the extent to which further integration of ASEAN itself to build an ASEAN community is also competing with domestic political challenges for its members' efforts and resources. In Northeast Asia, the survival of Cold War issues in the divided nations of China and Korea poses a major hindrance to community building as its effects transcend the parties directly involved.

Community building appears to be absent in the regional states' core national interests. In particular, countries in Southeast Asia have failed to define community building as part of their core national interests, leading them to persist in the practice of one-upmanship, which derails community building. This practice is evident in the reluctance shown by countries that occupy the chair of the ASEAN Standing Committee at any given time to share and consult with others regarding the initiatives to be taken during their tenure. The holding of the East Asia Summit in 2005, contrary to the recommendation of the EASG, is an important illustrative example in this regard. The challenge of harmonizing the EASG proposal for the East Asia Summit and the actual form of the summit as it has evolved since the 11th ASEAN Summit in December 2005 would not have arisen had Malaysia not launched the summit without prior consultation with its ASEAN partners.

One wonders if this might also be the case in the Plus Three countries. East Asia community building would have prospered much earlier had there been a willingness to make community building part of their national interests by desisting from actions that would undermine the common vision for East Asia that they had already agreed to in the EAVG and EASG reports.

Moreover, community building requires institutions. Too much flexibility and the excessive use of ad hoc arrangements are not conducive to community building. In East Asia, there is a general aversion toward institutions. In fact, China's interest in becoming part of the ASEAN process is in part due to ASEAN's informality and flexibility; the voluntary, nonbinding nature of commitments; and the absence of accountability for noncompliance.

Southeast Asia's performance record in institution building is also not very encouraging. ASEAN has moved very slowly over the past 40 years in this area, in part due to the jealous guarding of national sovereignty. The decision to establish an ASEAN Secretariat was made only in 1976—nine years after ASEAN's establishment and on the occasion of its first summit. That having been said, there is now a large window of opportunity before the grouping in the form of the drafting of the ASEAN Charter, a vehicle that ASEAN leaders understand to be a requirement for the realization of the ASEAN Community.

SOCIOECONOMIC OBSTACLES

Although ASEAN lost much of its economic competitiveness in large part due to the rise of China and other more attractive destinations for FDI, there has been some recovery in recent years, as FDI to ASEAN has begun to grow. The immediate loss of competitiveness compounded the effects of the Asian financial crisis by either halting or slowing down growth in Southeast Asia and inhibited the old ASEAN member states from doing more to level the economic divide between themselves and the newly admitted CLMV countries (Cambodia, Lao PDR, Myanmar, and Vietnam).

The remaining challenges include incomplete economic reforms, such as reforms of the monetary and financial systems and the proliferation of uncoordinated FTAs. Ten years after the crisis, there are concerns about unsustainable economic recovery, particularly if China's economic growth were to slow down, the US economy were to further decline, or Japan's recovery were to be short-lived. These scenarios point to the need to complete economic reforms to ensure the sustainability of economic recovery and growth. Also, while hopes were raised by the proliferation of FTAs in the region, there is also concern that they have become a "noodle bowl" whose lack of coordination might create further problems in the future. An argument that was raised earlier on is the need for a broad regional framework in which these various FTAs would fit without creating coordination and harmonization problems.

Moreover, elements of competition in their economies could pose an obstacle to community building, which requires cooperation rather than competition. While ASEAN should be pleased with Vietnam's economic performance, for example, there is concern among economies that are not doing as well about being overtaken by Vietnam. On the other hand, Vietnam's economic performance can be raised as a model for narrowing the ASEAN divide.

The difference in levels of economic development among the ASEAN+3 countries poses a real obstacle to community building. As already noted, community is best served by narrower differences in levels of economic development. This is the rationale for the EU's economic requirement for membership and the application of its cohesion funds to make the economies of candidate members more similar to those of the existing EU members. Vietnam has shown that the economic divide can be narrowed, although this can also act as a double-edged sword, as indicated above.

But the divide is even wider between most of the ASEAN countries on the one hand and the Plus Three countries on the other. Japan and South Korea are already members of the Organisation for Economic Cooperation and Development (OECD), the club of the wealthy that provides the bulk of the world's available resources for development. Most of East Asia remains the recipients of development assistance in spite of ASEAN's pre-crisis articulation of a transformation of its relations with its partners from a donor-donee relationship to a trade and investment partnership. The CLMV countries as well as Indonesia and the Philippines continue to require large amounts of ODA for their development. Despite multiyear double-digit economic growth since the 1980s, even China has not graduated to the status of a development assistance donor country just yet.

As a consequence of these different levels of economic development, there are wide income disparities and poverty within and across countries in East Asia.[3] These countries range from those with a relative absence of poverty, such as Japan, Singapore, South Korea, and Brunei, to those that in 2004 had a substantial percentage of their populations living on less than US$1 a day, such as Indonesia and Vietnam (7.5 percent), the Philippines (15.5 percent), China (16.6

3. The data on human development used in this section is from UNDP, *Human Development Report 2006—Beyond Scarcity: Power, Poverty and the Global Water Crisis* (New York: UNDP, 2006), available online at http://hdr.undp.org/hdr2006/.

percent), Lao PDR (27 percent), Myanmar (27 percent), and Cambodia (34.1 percent).

Related to this point is the fact that there exist huge differences in the level of human development across East Asia. The United Nations Development Programme's (UNDP) human development index (HDI) consists of gross domestic product (GDP) per capita, life expectancy at birth, and adult literacy. Other data supplementing the HDI include figures on each country's commitment to health (resources, access, and services); water, sanitation, and nutritional status; maternal and child health; status in terms of leading global health crises and risks; survival rates (infant mortality, maternal mortality, life expectancy); commitment to education (public spending); literacy and school enrollment; technology diffusion and creation; economic performance; inequality in income and expenditures; trade structure; rich country responsibilities (aid, debt relief, trade); flows of aid, private capital, and debt; priorities in public spending; energy and environment; refugees; armaments; victims of crime; the gender-related development index (GDI); gender inequality in education; and gender inequality in economic activity.

Of the 177 countries evaluated in terms of the HDI using 2004 data, Japan was ranked number 7, Singapore 25, South Korea 26, Brunei 34, and Malaysia 61—values indicating high development. Thailand was ranked number 74, China 81, the Philippines 84, Indonesia 108, Vietnam 109, Cambodia 129, Myanmar 130, and Lao PDR 133—values indicating medium development. Fortunately, none of the countries of East Asia remained in the low development group.

But it is in the disaggregated data relating to human development where the real disparities can be seen. Life expectancy at birth in 2004 ranged from Japan's 82.2 years to Lao PDR's 55.1 years, while GDP per capita ranged from Japan's US$29,251 (purchasing power parity, or PPP) to Lao PDR's US$1,954 (PPP). The Gini index, showing income inequality within countries, ranged from Japan's 24.9 to Cambodia's 40.4, Malaysia's 49.3, and China's 44.7, with the value of 0 representing perfect equality and 100 perfect inequality. With regard to the GDI, the range for East Asia is represented by Japan's 0.942 and Lao PDR's 0.545, placing them 13th and 100th respectively out of 136 countries evaluated by the UNDP. That the GDI is uneven within countries is seen by China's 0.761 GDI and rank of 64, while Hong Kong (SAR) has a GDI of 0.928 and a rank of 21.

The narrowing of the human development divide is therefore a major obstacle to community building in East Asia, particularly because the indicators of human development relate more directly to people than other socioeconomic obstacles, and because community, in the final analysis, is about people.

OVERCOMING THE OBSTACLES TO EAST ASIA COMMUNITY

The political obstacles to building an East Asia community can be redressed with time and with the political commitment of the leaders of ASEAN and East Asia. The dynamics of economic development will open up opportunities for the growth of middle classes with greater access to education, travel, and more and alternative information. In short, they will become more empowered individuals whose obedience to rulers of whatever kind can no longer be taken for granted in part because the rulers' erstwhile monopoly of the sources of information will have been broken. This could lead to political development of the regional states toward greater participation, observance of the rule of law, justice, and human rights. To ensure that the economic, social, and political transformation that follows economic growth and development does not undermine political stability, leaders of East Asia's states need to strategize and calibrate policy instruments and measures proactively and skillfully. Authoritarian rulers in the region must preside over their own demise in order to ensure a smoother transition in which economic growth unleashes social and political forces no longer governable under the old political arrangements.

In Southeast Asia, the ASEAN Community envisioned in the Bali Concord II could help redress these political obstacles if it receives the political commitment of leaders. Particularly relevant are the various elements of the ASEAN Security Community, including the shaping and sharing of norms and political development, where increased popular participation in governance, democracy, and human rights are promoted across ASEAN societies. That, together with institutional mechanisms that would help realize such a security community, including the ASEAN Charter as already stressed above, could go far in overcoming the existing and potential political obstacles.

The socioeconomic obstacles can also be redressed with time and political commitment on the part of the region's leaders. In Southeast Asia, the vehicle already exists in the form of the ASEAN Economic

Community and the ASEAN Socio-Cultural Community. Leaders throughout the region put a high premium on economic development, which can be sped up through greater economic cooperation and integration. Economic growth provides the resources by which human development can be improved, while both contribute to political legitimacy, especially for societies that do not have mechanisms for procedural legitimacy. The imperative for community building through economic integration is therefore strong, and this phenomenon is already taking place in East Asia.

CONCLUSION

The East Asia community can be advanced in spite of these obstacles through enhanced cooperation not only within ASEAN, but also among the ASEAN+3 countries. The shared vision for the region is already articulated in the EAVG report, and the broad strokes of this vision, as articulated in the medium- and short-term measures proposed by the EASG, are already guiding East Asia cooperation and integration. In addition, 2007 marked the adoption of the ASEAN+3 statement on enhanced cooperation over the next ten years, which provides more specific steps for realizing the East Asia community.

The obstacles can be overcome. However, as the EU experience has shown, as long as residual obstacles stand in the way and the trust and confidence deficit among participating states remains, the process will not be easy or smooth, the path will not be linear, and it will take an evolutionary, step-by-step approach.

Perhaps at the end of the day, the progress likely to occur in terms of economic and human development will unleash new social forces. If this happens, states may be overtaken by nonstate actors, driving the momentum of community building faster than state actors can cope with it. People-to-people interactions of all kinds—economic, cultural, professional, personal, and others outside the pale of state sovereignty—are already on the rise, and these are important building blocks for East Asia community. I will close, then, on this hopeful note, a statement of faith on what people are capable of achieving if they set their hearts and minds to it, either because they want it or because of strong imperatives that can only be ignored at their own peril.

4

Whither East Asia? Political Will and East Asian Regionalism

QIN YAQING

In November 2004, the leaders of ASEAN, China, Japan, and South Korea accepted a proposal put forth by the East Asia Vision Group (EAVG) and agreed to make the building of an East Asia community their long-term goal. This decision represented great progress in the regional process, showing the determination of these nations to work for peace, stability, and prosperity through community building.

Then, in 2005, the first East Asia Summit was held in Malaysia with the participation of 16 countries, including the ten ASEAN nations, the "Plus Three" nations (China, Japan, and South Korea), Australia, New Zealand, and India. That summit marked a further step forward in the process of East Asian regionalism, providing an important forum for strategic dialogue. At the same time, the ASEAN+3 process has continued to move forward, serving as the main vehicle for East Asian regional integration and for carrying out numerous cooperative activities in a wide range of functional fields.[1]

East Asian regionalism has been making significant progress, yet it now stands at a crossroads. On the one hand, there are strong dynamics that have been pushing regional cooperation forward and encouraging

1. See the two declarations adopted at the first East Asia Summit at www.aseansec.org/18098.htm and www.aseansec.org/18101.htm.

nations in the region to produce new initiatives and ideas. Many used to believe that the 1997 financial crisis would derail East Asian regional economic development, but in fact the post-crisis dynamic has provided even stronger impetus, encouraging the continued growth of the region. On the other hand, serious obstacles exist. Many of these have been brought up over the past few years—for example, the enormous diversity in the region, the low level of institutionalization, and the lack of spillover effects from economic cooperation to other fields. Disagreements also exist: opinions have differed both before and after the first East Asia Summit, and people have debated such questions as whether East Asia should have a geographical limit and how outside players should participate in the regional process, although everyone seems to agree on the need for open regionalism.[2]

Underlying all these arguments and disagreements is one question: "Whither East Asia?" Undoubtedly, East Asian regionalism has scored remarkable successes, but at the same time it is faced with uncertainty. Opportunities and challenges stand side by side.

REGIONAL COOPERATION: PROGRESS AND PROBLEMS

East Asia as a region first showed itself to the world in 1996, when ASEAN, China, Japan, and South Korea together started an official dialogue with the European Union (EU), namely the Asia-Europe Meeting.[3] The awareness of the importance of regional cooperation was increasing at that time, and East Asia entered a new era of regional integration following the 1997 Asian financial crisis, which highlighted the importance of cooperation and enhanced the sense of a common fate among East Asian nations. Because of the seriousness and urgency of the crisis, leaders of the ASEAN nations, and of China, Japan, and South Korea, met in Kuala Lumpur to discuss how to deal with the crisis through joint efforts. Thus, 1997 marked the initiation of the East Asian regional process, which is characterized by cooperation in dealing with economic threats throughout the region.

---

2. Yeo Lay Hwee, "The Nature and Future of East Asian Regionalism," in *Emerging East Asian Regionalism: Trend and Response*, ed. Zhang Yunling and Wang Fan (Beijing: World Affairs Press, 2005).
3. Zhang Yunling, "New Regionalism and East Asian Community Building," in *Emerging East Asian Regionalism*, 3.

The 1997–2005 period can be termed the first stage of East Asian regionalism, a period marked by the rapid development of economic and functional cooperation among nations within the ASEAN+3 framework. During these years, rapid and dynamic progress was made in terms of regional economic integration. These nations, which came together initially to mitigate risks, were now striving for a community of lasting peace, prosperity, and progress. Since the process began, the dynamic has been stronger than expected.

The year 2005 saw the beginning of the second stage of East Asian regionalism with the convening of the first East Asia Summit. Yet this is a stage in which new uncertainties have surfaced. At present, there are both opportunities and challenges in furthering regional cooperation. Outstanding achievements have been made in economic and non-traditional security cooperation and in institution building; at the same time, however, there are still many practical difficulties in all of these areas. This section offers an analytical review of the current situation in East Asian regional cooperation.

Economic Cooperation: Dynamic but Inadequately Integrated

In the last ten years, economic cooperation in East Asia has been dynamic. Since the 1997 Asian financial crisis, regional economic cooperation has expanded from 6 to 16 economies, and the areas of cooperation have continuously broadened. East Asia has become the fastest-growing region in the world, now accounting for approximately 20 percent of the global economy, and the nations in the region are bound by increasingly close economic ties.

Intraregional trade development has been marked by the proliferation of free trade agreements (FTAs). In 2005, intraregional trade accounted for almost half of the region's total. The first steps toward creating an FTA that would cover all ASEAN nations were taken in 2002, with the start of the ASEAN FTA, which is intended to be the basis for the development of an integrated ASEAN market by 2020. Bilateral FTA negotiations between ASEAN and its partners are also underway and have shown step-by-step progress and promising results. China serves as a good example. In 2002, the China-ASEAN Framework Agreement on Comprehensive Economic Cooperation was reached, which stipulated that a China-ASEAN FTA would be completed by 2010. Since then, the Early Harvest Program, a 2004 corollary FTA to reduce tariffs on certain agricultural and other products; the Agreement on Trade in Goods (2004); and the Agreement on Trade in Services (2007) have been launched or signed, one after the other. This has greatly facilitated the FTA process. South Korea and Japan are also expected to conclude FTA arrangements with ASEAN in 2009 and 2012 respectively.

East Asian financial cooperation has made headway as well, particularly in terms of the ASEAN Swap Arrangements that were outlined in the Chiang Mai Initiative, and in terms of the Asian Bond Markets Initiative. Since it was officially launched in 2001, the Chiang Mai mechanism has seen significant expansion, with the total scale of swap arrangements reaching almost US$80 billion.[4] And post–Chiang Mai Initiative cooperation is moving ahead, as was clearly indicated by the agreement among the ASEAN+3 finance ministers to a reserve pooling arrangement, an important step toward multilateralization.[5] Driven by the Asian Bond Markets Initiative and the Asian Bond Fund, the overall size of the bond markets in East Asian economies (excluding Japan), expanded by 14 percent in 2005, the share of local currency bonds increased from 13 percent to more than 19 percent, and the Asian Bond Fund II officially started operations with a capacity of US$2 billion. Moreover, efforts are being made to study the possibility of and conditions for an Asian Currency Unit. This is of course a long-term goal, but once realized, it could be a significant advance in regional monetary cooperation.

In addition, East Asian investment cooperation has been catching up. In 2005, the combined foreign direct investment (FDI) from ten East Asian economies to Mainland China accounted for 58.6 percent of the latter's utilized FDI. In the same year, FDI from Japan to eight East Asian economies, including Mainland China, amounted to US$15.75 billion.[6]

Despite these achievements, however, economic cooperation faces a number of difficulties and practical problems as we enter the second stage of East Asian regionalism. The most prominent problem is that economic cooperation is not really integrated regionwide. In many

4. For an overview of the current status of the network of bilateral swap arrangements under the Chiang Mai Initiative, see www.mof.go.jp/english/if/CMI_0704.pdf.
5. Naris Chaiyasoot, "Assessment of the Latest Development of East Asian Financial Cooperation" (conference paper, NEAT Conference on East Asian Financial Cooperation, Shanghai, April 7–8, 2007).
6. Jiang Ruiping, "Positive Interaction between China's Economic Growth and East Asian Economic Cooperation," *Foreign Affairs Review* no. 15 (2006): 15.

cases, we see a combination of bilateral arrangements instead of one integrated multilateral framework. There are reasons for this, one of which is the development gap among East Asian economies. Economies at different development levels vary in their capacities and expectations for economic cooperation, which certainly hinders the integration process of the region. Also, there is a relatively high degree of similarity in economic structures among East Asian nations, which causes rather serious competition in their exports as well as in attracting FDI. Looking at financial cooperation, for example, ten years after the 1997 financial crisis we find that the amount of volatile, short-term foreign capital, or "hot money," in East Asia is even greater and still lacks effective surveillance and utilization; the financial systems in the East Asian nations are still vulnerable; bond markets remain underdeveloped; and intraregional exchange rate coordination is still far from adequate.

However, the most important reason for the lack of an integrated framework is perhaps the inadequate political will and lack of coordination among China, Japan, and South Korea. Since these three countries account for 90 percent of East Asia's total gross domestic product, the region can hardly be economically integrated without their coordinated efforts.

Security Cooperation: Urgently Needed but Conspicuously Unbalanced

East Asian security cooperation is mostly carried out in nontraditional security areas, triggered and facilitated by the growing prominence of such critical issues as infectious diseases, natural disasters, and terrorism. In 1999, China, Japan, and South Korea started sharing information on environmental protection, earthquake early warning and forecasting, and transnational crime, and this has yielded positive outcomes so far. Cooperation has also been enhanced under the ASEAN+3 framework in strengthening environmental protection; fighting communicable diseases such as severe acute respiratory syndrome, or SARS, and avian influenza; and responding to devastating natural disasters such as earthquakes and tsunamis. In 2004, ASEAN+3 held its first Ministerial Meeting on Transnational Crime, taking a concrete step toward nontraditional security cooperation. In 2005, ASEAN+3 signed the Beijing Declaration to strengthen coordination and cooperation among member nations' police forces. At the 12th ASEAN Summit, held in January

2007, the leaders agreed to get tougher on terror. And at the second East Asia Summit, held immediately after the ASEAN Summit, member states adopted the Cebu Declaration on East Asian Energy Security, demonstrating their commitment to ensuring energy security in the region. Cooperation in the nontraditional security areas has thus been dynamic and fruitful.

In comparison, cooperation in the field of traditional security has lagged far behind. Perhaps the 2002 signing of the Declaration on the Conduct of Parties in the South China Sea can be regarded as one of the few examples of cooperation on traditional security. To some degree, the signing of the Treaty of Amity and Cooperation in Southeast Asia also shows at least a willingness by member states to cooperate in areas of traditional security. East Asian states also cooperate under other frameworks, such as the ASEAN Regional Forum and the Six-Party Talks. The recent achievements of the latter dialogue are encouraging, although the road ahead is still long and rough. Because of these efforts, East Asia has been fairly stable and the most serious problems and risks in the region are relatively under control.

In short, we have seen the unbalanced development so far in terms of cooperation in the fields of traditional and nontraditional security. One important reason for this imbalance is the lack of mutual political trust. Because of historical issues; territorial disputes; and differences in political systems, ideologies, religions, and cultures, it is difficult for states in the region to dispel doubts and suspicions toward each other. Without a sufficient level of trust, it is impossible to build a collective identity, which is critical for a community in the traditional security sense. Moreover, East Asia is a region in which the big powers have complicated strategic interests. Some other elements and mechanisms are also at play. For instance, the hub-and-spokes system that the United States set up during the Cold War years still has a significant impact on regional peace and stability. Under such circumstances, substantive cooperation on traditional security is a complicated issue indeed.

Institution Building: Plenty of Mechanisms but a Low Level of Institutionalization

Since the 1997 Asian financial crisis, various regional cooperation mechanisms have been established at different levels and have provided important platforms for the smooth implementation of cooperative measures in a number of areas. The main vehicle for East Asian cooperation and East Asia community building is ASEAN+3, which actually includes mechanisms at the ASEAN+3, ASEAN+1, ASEAN, and Plus-Three levels. In the last decade, ASEAN+3 has produced great achievements in institution building. ASEAN+3 Summits have been held regularly with the participation of heads of state and governments from around the region since 1997. Beyond that, however, ASEAN+3 covers more than 18 sectors, comprises 50 bodies, and includes more than a dozen ministerial meetings and even more director-general meetings. In short, ASEAN+3 has become "a web of cooperation spanning the cultural, economic, functional, political, security, and social areas."[7]

The East Asia Summit is another significant outcome of institution building in the region. As a strategic forum with external countries, it has become a positive supplement to the ASEAN+3 mechanism and an important contributor to East Asia community building. In addition, there are many subregional arrangements and quite a few Track II mechanisms that are playing increasingly important roles in regional cooperation.[8]

However, despite the great number of high-level meetings, the level of institutionalization of the cooperation mechanisms and arrangements in East Asia is quite low. Many of them are limited to information exchange and expressions of goodwill and are therefore not very effective in producing tangible results. It seems that there is a lack of strong incentives for institution building even though there has been a lot of rhetoric. To institutionalists, ASEAN+3 is not a formal institution based on legal-rationalistic foundations but merely a cooperative framework or loose arrangement. It is often criticized for its lack of structure, formal agenda, or clear format for decision-making procedures and implementation.[9] Such a low level of institutionalization may have increased the comfort level and helped maintain the integration process, but it does not encourage further progress toward institutionalization and in fact loosens the efficiency and effectiveness of cooperation.

7. Ong Keng Yong, "Foreword," in *ASEAN+3 Documents Series 1999-2004*, ed. ASEAN Secretariat (Jakarta: ASEAN, 2005).
8. Su Hao, "Regional Institutional Building in the Process of East Asian Regional Cooperation," in *East Asian Cooperation and Sino-American Relations*, ed. Zhu Liqun and Wang Fan (Beijing: World Affairs Press, 2006).
9. David Shambaugh, "The Evolving Asian System: A New Regional Structure?" (conference paper, East Asia Cooperation and Sino-US Relations Conference, Beijing, China, November 3–4, 2005).

This low level of institutionalization is often defined as one of the characteristic features of East Asian regionalism. It is sometimes called the "ASEAN way" or the "Asian way." A comparative study of East Asia and Europe has pointed out the differences between the two regions. European regionalism is legalistically based and politically motivated, while East Asian regionalism is informally oriented and economically motivated.[10] It is true that because of the different regional dynamic and institutional order, East Asia cannot—and need not—be a copy of the EU. However, a sufficient level of regional institutionalization is needed if a region is to implement measures aimed at closer cooperation and the building of a community.

In sum, East Asian regionalism has made progress in all areas. In the political and security areas, the nations that have joined this regional process have not had military conflicts with one another. Even though many issues—especially territorial disputes—are yet to be solved, settlement through negotiation and dialogue seems to be accepted by most as the norm for behavior. The original five countries of ASEAN have not fought against each other since 1967, when the Bangkok Declaration was signed; the ASEAN 10 have not fought against each other since the ASEAN expansion; and the ASEAN+3 countries have not fought against each other since they became involved in the regional process. In nontraditional security areas, many mechanisms have been set up to deal with common problems and challenges. Energy security and conservation, public health, natural disasters, and environmental protection are all considered to be areas for strengthened cooperation. China and Japan, for example, have cooperated on many of these issues in recent years, even as the two countries were experiencing difficult times in their bilateral relations. Economic cooperation has been extremely dynamic as well, as joint efforts have been made and great successes achieved in trade, finance, and investment.

Given this peculiar situation in which East Asian nations are building a community while a Westphalian culture still dominates in the region, the achievements made to date in promoting the ideal of an East Asia community are even more remarkable. But at the same time, given this situation, we should not be surprised that disagreements on important regional issues have been surfacing and are looming larger than before.

---

10. Peter Katzenstein, *A World of Regions: Asia and Europe in the American Imperium* (Ithaca: Cornell University, 2005).

BUILDING A COMMUNITY OUT OF A WESTPHALIAN CULTURE

It is precisely now, when all this progress has been made, that East Asia faces new choices. It can go forward toward further regional integration and realize the ultimate goal of building a regional community. It can meander around the crossroads, maintaining a low level of functional cooperation without a further deepening of regional integration. Or it could even move backward toward a relationship of more suspicion and hostility among nations in the region. All the possibilities are there. If the region does not move forward, however, it is quite possible that it will move backward.

The key to whether the region moves forward or backward lies in the political will of all parties, which lags far behind the dynamic regional processes of economic and functional cooperation. Many have compared East Asia to Europe. If that comparison tells us anything, it is that there are conspicuous differences between the regional cultures. In particular, it highlights the fact that East Asia is still dominated by a Westphalian culture, which lies behind the lack of political will.

There are several features that characterize a Westphalian culture. First, there is a strong sense of sovereignty.[11] Almost every nation in this region is highly sensitive to national sovereignty and takes it as the property that protects the state and enables it to live and prosper. Two important factors play a particularly significant role in this respect. One is the recent history of the region. Colonization and aggression before and during World War II and hostility and confrontation during the Cold War have formed the recent memories of the Asian nations. It is therefore natural that many consider independence to be precious and view sovereignty—a Western concept and the most important principle in the modern international system—as crucial for protecting their national interest. The other factor, related to the first, is the sensitivity to territory. Unresolved territorial disputes among many of the countries in the region heighten this sensitivity. Related to that is the rise of irrational nationalism in various countries, which adds to both the sovereignty- and territory-related sensitivities.

A second feature is that military power is a highly sensitive issue for a Westphalian culture with the state at its center. The military strength of a

---

11. Amitav Acharya, *Constructing a Security Community in Southeast Asia* (London: Routledge, 2001).

nation-state is seen as the most important means to guarantee its survival and to protect its interests because the regional system, as well as the international system, is anarchic. Although nations can gain a lot through cooperation, a Westphalian man is always worried about how much more others may gain in cooperation and about whether the gain by others will be used against him in the future.[12] Power, and especially military power, is therefore always at the forefront of his mind. As a result, nations are sensitive to the growth of overall capabilities in general and military might in particular.

In addition to the concern about growing power in the region—especially that of China—there is also the worry about the military alliances with the United States. The hub-and-spokes alliance structure in East Asia, including the formal US military alliances with Japan, South Korea, the Philippines, and Thailand, and the informal US alliance with Singapore, continues to exist as the dominant security framework in Asia, but some believe that US dominance has been declining and that US allies may no longer consider US interests a priority. Some even argue that the United States may be excluded from the region mainly because the rise of China will change the regional power structure.[13] Concern about hard power, therefore, reflects distrust among the nations in the region as well as worries on the side of the United States.

Third, the East Asian regional process is primarily a government-dominated process. It is true that regional cooperation in East Asia has been driven by economic need. However, in East Asia, the state has been strong and society weak, especially compared with Europe, resulting in a state-dominated regional program. Since the 1997 East Asian financial crisis, the governments in this region have realized that they need to cooperate to better meet the challenges and reduce the risks brought about by globalization, and that they should work together on the basis of common interests. Thus, most of the regional programs and initiatives have been started by governments.

For a community, however, sharing a popular society and a sense of identity is important. It is clear that economic cooperation has brought great

12. Joseph Grieco, "Anarchy and the Limits of Cooperation: A Realist Critique of the Newest Liberal Institutionalism," in *Neorealism and Neoliberalism: The Contemporary Debate*, ed. David Baldwin (New York: Columbia University Press, 1993), 116–140.

13. Michael Yahuda, "East Asian Cooperation: Prospects and Challenges" (conference paper, East Asia Cooperation and Sino-US Relations Conference, Beijing, China, November 3–4, 2005); US-China Economic and Security Review Commission Report to Congress (July 2002).

benefits to peoples in the region in the past decade. Communication and exchange have been strengthened thanks to the efforts made by all nations in East Asia. But it would be a mistake to believe that geographical proximity can naturally bring about mutual understanding and trust. Sometimes we may live in close proximity but know little about each other. Since East Asia's regionalism has a very short history and since the efforts have mostly focused on economic growth, the level of people-to-people exchange is far from sufficient. The fact that nationalism has been on the rise in the region is an indication of the inadequacy of efforts to date to build a common culture and sense of community among the people of the region.

The Westphalian culture means that tensions exist between the effort to build a regional community and worries about each other's intentions in doing so, between a dynamic and profitable regional process and uncertainties about each other's intentions and future orientation. Considering these factors, we have to admit that the East Asian nations have made remarkable progress in the last ten years. But while community building is moving ahead against the Westphalian background, at the same time we need to see clearly that the Westphalian culture does have a strong impact at this crucial juncture and that disagreements exist as to how to build this community.

DISAGREEMENTS ON APPROACHES TO AN EAST ASIA COMMUNITY

The efforts to build a regional community, while enormous, have been accompanied by all the considerations that naturally emerge within a Westphalian culture, as described above. Thus, when there are tangible common interests, cooperation gains dynamism; when the Westphalian concerns conflict with community-building efforts, political will becomes diluted and hesitation dominates. This is a most serious dilemma as East Asia reaches a crossroads. Since the first East Asia Summit, a number of disagreements have emerged, further reflecting the dilemma facing this region.

Disagreement on the Definition of the Region

In the years since the decision to hold an East Asia Summit, a debate has been going on as to how to define the region. There are primarily two different schools of thought. Some argue that the region has been clearly defined by the EAVG as including only ASEAN+3, and they believe that deepening is more important than widening at present. Others, however, believe that the definition of the region should expand to include other nations such as India, Australia, New Zealand, and more. In 2001, for example, then Japanese Prime Minister Koizumi put forward the idea of an "enlarged East Asia community," which would include Australia and New Zealand.[14]

The insistence on ASEAN+3 is based on the belief that certain geographical limits should be set to make the process effective and substantial. The advocacy of expansion and the inclusion of outside powers to establish a larger region, on the other hand, might be based on political considerations rather than a mere geographical consideration.[15] The disagreement seems to be one of different approaches and ideas about how East Asian regionalism should go forward. At the same time, it perhaps implies a consideration of power relations in the region, for example balancing a rising China or maintaining a certain balance of power. Although the first East Asia Summit was held after all sides had agreed with the ASEAN consensus on its membership, the disagreement has only been shelved rather than solved.

Disagreement on the Leading Force for the Regional Process

East Asian regionalism has been led by ASEAN, the group of small and medium-sized nations that started the process and set up its rules and norms.[16] Since 1997, the process has been enlarged to include China, Japan, and South Korea, and the ASEAN+3 mechanism was thus created. That new mechanism, however, has been accompanied by a debate as to who should lead the process. Some argue that the European integration process has been successful because two major powers on the European continent, namely France and Germany, have played a crucial role and provided the leadership. The situation in East Asia differs from Europe in that it lacks effective leaders. With the involvement of the "Plus Three" countries, should China, Japan, or South Korea, or the three together, play the leading role?

---

14. Qin Hausun, Wang Shunzhu, and Gu Yuanyang, eds., *Roadmap for Asian Regional Cooperation* (Beijing: Shishi Press, 2006), 49.
15. Katzenstein, *A World of Regions*, 6–13.
16. Acharya, *Constructing a Security Community*.

With the holding of the East Asia Summit in 2005, the leadership debate moved beyond a mere argument about the lack of major power leadership. Now that the two processes, ASEAN+3 and the East Asia Summit, are moving ahead together in the region, what functions and roles should they play respectively? The East Asia Summit, which includes Australia, New Zealand, and India, seems to illustrate the very nature of East Asia's open regionalism.[17] ASEAN+3, on the other hand, continues to develop more substantive cooperation among a smaller group of members. At the ASEAN+3 Summit and the East Asia Summit in 2005, the roles of these mechanisms were defined respectively as being the main vehicle for community building and a forum for strategic dialogue. But since that time, another round of debates has gotten underway, questioning which mechanism will play a more important role and whether the East Asia Summit should be strengthened to provide the major platform for regional community building.

Thus, the leadership debate has been moving along two tracks: one focuses on which player or players should lead, while the other centers on which process, ASEAN+3 or the East Asia Summit, should play a more important role in the regional process. The debate is far from over.

Disagreement on Institutionalization

As discussed above, East Asian regionalism is characterized by its low level of institutionalization and informality.[18] Over the past several decades, this informal style—the "ASEAN way"—has helped to bring together nations in the region and to maintain the process of prosperity and progress. Especially in light of the complexity and diversity that exist in almost every aspect of life in East Asia, it is fair to say that without following the ASEAN way to some extent, it would have been impossible for East Asian nations to cooperate so successfully.

However, along with the rapid development of East Asian regionalism, and particularly with the decision made by the ASEAN+3 leaders to make the building of an East Asia community their long-term goal, the question of institutionalization has arisen again as an important topic.

---

17. The conditions for participation are that these countries must 1) join the Treaty of Amity and Cooperation or have agreed to join it, 2) be a formal ASEAN dialogue partner, and 3) have substantive cooperative relations with ASEAN.

18. Acharya, *Constructing a Security Community.*

On the one hand, some believe that the low level of institutionalization in the East Asian regional process is more beneficial because it has managed to work and because East Asian cultural characteristics are unique. On the other hand, some warn that European regionalism has succeeded because it is rules based and thus stress that East Asian regionalism should be more institutionalized.[19] When East Asian regionalism was in its early stages, a loose arrangement was more beneficial, but as it continues to develop, it will require more formal institutions to provide a binding effect on the nations concerned. The ASEAN Secretariat has complained many times that the low level of institutionalization makes the implementation of ASEAN+3 Summit decisions and other important measures extremely difficult. While the Europeans have produced one treaty after another, Asians prefer to have declarations that do not have a strong binding force. On the surface, the present disagreement over institutionalization is about whether a high level of institutionalization will create a democratic deficit as is thought to have happened in Europe, but the underlying worry is perhaps more about the erosion of national sovereignty.

Disagreement on Areas for Cooperation

There is a de facto disagreement over the areas in which nations should cooperate, although all sides have expressed a willingness to have wide-ranging cooperation. The consensus is that cooperation should be carried out in whichever areas are easiest, implying that in some areas, such as traditional security, cooperation is still very difficult. So far, the majority of the cooperation has occurred in terms of economic and functional issues, and it is in these areas too that the greatest progress has been made to date. It is very difficult, however, to have any spillover effect from successful cooperation in these areas to highly political issues.

European regionalism's greatest achievement is that it has made war among the European nations "not merely unthinkable, but materially impossible."[20] For this purpose, the Europeans have built up their institutions in both functional and political areas. East Asian regionalism differs in that it was initiated as a result of urgent economic needs. Considering the security problems the

---

19. Qin, Wang, and Gu, *Roadmap for Asian Regional Cooperation*, 54–55.
20. Robert Schuman's "Schuman Declaration" (May 9, 1950) can be found online at www.europa.eu/abc/symbols/9-may/decl_en.htm.

nations face in East Asia, multilateral frameworks for traditional security cooperation are not easy to come by, even though everyone seems to agree that the Korean nuclear issue endangers regional security and that some multilateral framework is needed to maintain peace and stability.

These disagreements show that a consensus on the roadmap for building an East Asia community is yet to be reached. Sometimes, we use the European model as a term of reference, but in fact the East Asian approach is very different mainly because of the clear existence of a Westphalian aspect to regional interactions. Some may argue that Europe five decades ago was in a similar, or even worse, position in some regards. But one thing is worth particular attention: European regionalism, which was supported by the United States, started after World War II, when the European nations were all allies and needed only to overcome the historical legacies. In Asia today, we have both bitter memories of the past and strong levels of distrust about each other's intentions in the present to overcome, while the United States is somewhat suspicious and hesitant. This is a fact to deal with and not something to complain about. These disagreements reflect the tenaciousness of the Westphalian culture that has existed in the region. If we are to overcome these difficulties and realize the goal of building a community, our political will must be stronger than the tension produced by the region's Westphalian culture.

POLITICAL WILL AND A SUSTAINABLE REGIONAL PROCESS

East Asian regionalism is still in the initial stages and remains quite weak. Considering the presence of a Westphalian culture in this region, it is natural to have disagreements—and more can be expected. We must admit this fact and realize that it is impossible to change this overnight. The crucial question at present is how to maintain the momentum on the one hand and reduce the intensity of the Westphalian culture on the other, thereby relaxing the tension between the two. We must amass sufficient political will to at least maintain the momentum of regional cooperation and integration. In this regard, there are a number of measures that are important to the further progress of East Asian regionalism.

First, the regional cooperation process must be maintained. Since East Asia has neither a strong legalistic foundation like Europe nor a clear power structure like North America, East Asian multilateral regionalism is primarily process oriented. More often than not, keeping the process going is the most important work facing the region. There are complaints that the East Asian regional process often fails to produce tangible results and that therefore the various mechanisms continue to be like so much loose sand. But we must remember that the process itself is of great significance, for the process of building an East Asia community is valuable for confidence building and suspicion reduction, for the creation and learning of norms, and for the expansion of common interests and convergence of expectations. Only by maintaining the process at this initial stage can we hope to achieve tangible results in the future.

To say that the process matters does not merely imply that the process is important because the rules and norms (both regulatory and constitutive) that it produces matter; rather, it also means that often the process itself is the focus. Once nations are involved in the process, they are integrating and being integrated. Therefore, "process maintenance" in East Asian multilateral regionalism is often more important than producing results. For East Asia, where diversity is so conspicuous and where small and medium-sized nations hope to "socialize" major powers through regional community building, the regional process itself is often the end as well as the means. It is the process that has woven a regional web, entangling all concerned as stakeholders. This attention to process maintenance and trust building may be called "soft institutionalism."

Second, integration rather than containment or balancing should be the way to achieve a community. Very often, words like balancing or containment come to mind and the Westphalian culture makes this inclination even more pronounced. Especially in light of China's rapid development, various concepts of balancing have emerged, and policies made by countries in the region are sometimes influenced by such ideas. But balancing China (or India, in a similar sense) is highly risky. China is not the Cold War Soviet Union and is hard to define as an enemy. It is China's own will to join the process, and the changing identity of China serves as an important variable that has made the region more stable and prosperous than before. China's rapid development has provided more opportunities for the nations in the region. Australia, for example, hopes to join the regional process for the gains it can make from the strong economic dynamic rather than as a way of balancing China. Integration is a vastly preferable means to build a community, as the expansion of ASEAN to include Vietnam and Lao PDR has shown. Traditional strategic thinking with regard to balancing and counterbalancing would fail East Asian regionalism and push the region back to a Cold War scenario, a scenario that nobody would like to see.

Third, nations in this region should work harder to set up a regionwide FTA, or an East Asian FTA (EAFTA). The East Asian regional process was started with the specific purpose of dealing with the East Asian financial crisis. It was a common threat that made these nations aware of the importance of regional cooperation. Although this process did not have a clear political goal as the EU did in the early 1950s, cooperation aimed at economic development has produced norms and rules during the course of its evolution. Continued cooperative efforts in the economic arena are the most effective way to push the regional process forward, and the most effective measure is to work on the earlier completion of the EAFTA, which will produce greater benefits than will bilateral FTAs.

Fourth, major powers should exercise restraint. The political will to work together, to settle disputes through consultation and dialogue, and to make concessions if the regional process itself threatens to be derailed must be the norm we follow. In this respect, self-restraint on the part of the major players is indispensable. The agreement that ASEAN should take the leading role and sit in the driver's seat is not mere rhetoric. In a Westphalian culture, suspicion among major powers could doom regional cooperation. Neither China nor Japan, for example, can take the lead, for it could start a malignant spiral of competition and increase the level of suspicion and distrust. Their self-restraint and support for the leading role of ASEAN is a practical measure to hold the regional process together. Community building, by definition, rejects the use of hard power while requiring the smart use of soft power and influence to move the process forward.

In this respect, relations between China and Japan are crucially important. In the past few years, voices at various conferences in the region have expressed concern about the relations between the two countries, as well as hope that China and Japan will improve relations. It is a general belief that tension and hostility between the two countries hinders regional cooperation. The visit of the Japanese prime minister to China in October 2006 and the joint statement by the leaders of the two countries were good signs, and the visit of the Chinese premier to

Japan in April 2007 brought further improvement, but relations are still very fragile. Competition between China and Japan for regional leadership could destroy East Asian regionalism. In addition, major actors outside of the region need to show their political will to support a healthy regional process. Unfortunately, neither the United States nor Europe seems to have come up with a clear policy toward East Asian regionalism.

Fifth, within the region itself, public awareness of and popular support for the building of an East Asia community must be strengthened. The political will of nations in the region is not only reflected in their regional policy but also in their domestic arenas. If the building of the East Asia community is to be sustainable, it cannot be an elite program forever. Strong political will is needed to raise public awareness and gain popular support so that a more favorable environment can be created and sociocultural ties enhanced among peoples across the region. This will lead nations to go beyond the mere calculation of their immediate gain from the process and enable them to develop a sense of "we-ness" and of community identity. In this respect, more attention should be paid to young people in the region. Since the East Asia community is a long-term goal, it is important to nurture friendship and trust among the young, who will carry the cause forward.

CONCLUSION

East Asia is a dynamic region, and cooperation among its nations has been fruitful. The building of a regional community has been accepted as our long-term goal, but East Asian regionalism has now come to a crossroads. The answer to the question "Whither East Asia?" lies in the tension between inadequate political will—a result of the dominant Westphalian culture in the region—on the one hand and the strong dynamic that has propelled the regional process forward over the past decade on the other. At present, this tension is a most formidable obstacle to East Asia community building; whether the process of community building will continue or not depends very much on whether this obstacle can be overcome.

The recent improvement of Sino-Japanese relations shows what an important role political will can play in bilateral relations. At the same time, the disagreement on the definition of the region, the low level of institutionalization, and the sluggishness of the spillover effects all indicate that the political will is not up to expectations and falls short of the practical needs. It also shows that political will rests on the determination of politicians, the support of the people, and the nurturing effect of the regional process.

Just a few years ago, people had many doubts about an East Asia community. When the EAVG put forward the idea, it was even taken as a rosy dream. Today, it has become very much an accepted term and a common goal. This is why we should be optimistic about the region's future. At the same time, we need to understand that East Asian regionalism is weak and fragile, that the process is of ultimate importance at this stage of regional cooperation, and that great care should be taken to help the region progress toward a more peaceful and more prosperous East Asia.

As for the future development of East Asian regionalism, Jusuf Wanandi has identified two views, one pessimistic and the other optimistic. He discusses the latter view as follows:

> The more optimistic view is based on close observations of developments in East Asia, where efforts are being taken to establish new regional institutions. Obviously these observers are mostly from East Asia, and are not only following these developments closely but are also involved in the efforts . . . . They are optimistic because they see the great opportunity of, and are given the chance to participate in, an emerging East Asia that might become the center of development and progress in the mid-21st century.[21]

He is quite right. We must be optimistic, not only because we have made great achievements but also because we cannot miss this golden opportunity in the modern history of East Asia to build a community of peace, prosperity, and progress. The road ahead is still tortuous, but the future is very bright. Seizing this historic opportunity and achieving this vision will require greater political will if we are to overcome the region's Westphalian culture and push the process of East Asia community building forward.

---

21. Jusuf Wanandi, "Keynote Speech" (NEAT Conference on East Asian Financial Cooperation, Shanghai, April 7–8, 2007).

III

Strengthening the Foundations for East Asia Community

5

Expanding the Agenda for Regional Economic Cooperation

JESUS P. ESTANISLAO

The Asian financial crisis, which affected large swathes of the East Asian economic region slightly more than a decade ago, is remembered in a typically Asian manner. The enormous cost of the crisis is properly acknowledged. At the same time, the ability of the region to tap new opportunities, thereby enabling it to recover from the crisis is quietly celebrated.

Not only has the cost been counted in terms of amounts lost and resources spent in economic and financial restructuring, but it has also been reckoned in terms of the destabilization that inevitably spread from the economic and financial spheres into the political and social spheres. In some economies of the region, changes in government were unexpectedly accelerated as millions of citizens were swept back below the poverty line.

There can be no underestimating the cost of the Asian financial crisis. But neither can we close our eyes to the opportunities that virtually all economies in the region seized in trying to recover. With the hindsight that a decade now affords, it appears that the lights switched on by opportunities smartly seized look brighter than the shadows cast in the immediate aftermath of the crisis.

Indeed, there is hardly any talk in the region of a decade lost. Rather, much of the reference is to the remarkable recovery that the region has been able to stage. Looking at the region as a whole, real gross domestic product (GDP) has grown at an annual average rate of 9 percent. Export growth has been even higher, to the extent that the region now accounts for one-fifth of the global export volume.[1] Complemented by significant inflows of foreign direct investment (FDI) into the region, these export surpluses have enabled virtually all economies in the region to significantly boost their foreign exchange reserves.

Moreover, in contrast to what was seen in the immediate aftermath of the crisis, two positive developments need to be highlighted. First, in the decade since the onset of the Asian financial crisis, it is estimated that on a net basis, some 300 million people in the region have crossed back above the poverty line, offsetting the millions who were thrown below it at the start of the crisis. And second, the region is no longer a set of individual economies gasping for financial support from those outside the region. It has become much more integrated, giving greater substance to references to East Asia as one economic region. After all, intraregional trade now accounts for 54 percent of East Asia's total trade. This is admittedly still a shade below the 60 percent that the European Union (EU) claims, but it is already above the corresponding 45 percent for the North American Free Trade Agreement (NAFTA).[2]

Much of what has been achieved in the region can be traced to the remarkable economic performance of China. Its economy has been growing, generally at double-digit rates or at rates very close to double digits. China's ability to sell in export markets and to attract significant amounts of FDI has enabled it to build its exchange reserves to unparalleled heights. Looking up at those heights, other economies—particularly the United States and those in the EU as well—have been pressing China to allow its exchange rate to move accordingly. In the decade after the Asian financial crisis, China has loomed very large, not only in affecting the recovery of the entire East Asian region but also in shaping economic perceptions in global financial markets.

China's dramatic economic performance during the past decade has been phenomenal indeed. No other economy in the region or beyond comes anywhere close. But China has not been alone in growing its GDP and its export volume. Neither has it been alone in attracting FDI and in building foreign exchange reserves. Virtually all other economies in

---

1. Indermit Gill and Homi Kharas, *An East Asian Renaissance: Ideas for Economic Growth* (Washington DC: World Bank, 2007), 1.

2. Gill and Kharas, *An East Asian Renaissance*, 8.

the region have been following suit, in part being pulled up by China's economic dynamism.

All of the other economies in the East Asian region have been playing a part in driving the region forward. Through mainly market-driven policies, they have been able to achieve higher levels of GDP growth. And as a natural byproduct of higher GDP growth rates and of relatively more open trade regimes, they have been able to raise their export growth rates even more significantly. In the process, they too have been able to contribute to the much higher degree of regionalization in East Asia.

Japan, in particular, has been notable for its contribution to a higher degree of regionalization. Despite the much slower growth of the Japanese economy during this period, Japanese multinationals have still been able to play a very significant role in making East Asia a more cohesive economic region in the decade since the onset of the Asian financial crisis. Japanese multinationals have been sending as much as 80 percent of their exports from their East Asian affiliates to other countries in the region. And they have been sourcing as much as 95 percent of their imports from their affiliate plants elsewhere in East Asia.

East Asia, then, seems to have emerged from the financial crisis as a much more integrated region—to a point where referring to an East Asian economic region has almost as much substance as referring to the EU as one European economic region and, even more so, to NAFTA as one North American economic region. As described above, the higher level of regionalization in East Asia has been achieved mainly through intraregional trade, which has been facilitated by higher real economic growth, greater reliance on market-driven policies, and more open trade regimes.

In this light, the dream of eventually building an East Asia community, initially through more free and open trade, has been gradually realized in the past decade. The tentative arrangements for more free and open trade in the region that were put in place in a fashion that can be described as almost gingerly—starting with ASEAN and more recently extending ASEAN to include other East Asian economies—seem to have survived the skepticism generally heaped on them. These arrangements may yet provide a useful framework and one of several venues for efforts to bring the regionalization in East Asia to a much higher level.

The Foundation and Context for Further Regionalization in East Asia

Having been brought to a fork in the road by the Asian financial crisis, the economies of the region could have chosen to go down the road of putting up barriers and closing themselves off from the crosscurrents of more open economic interaction with each other and with the rest of the world. To their credit, they chose instead to move along the road toward freer and more open trade. The choice may not have been easy for a few economies in the region. But it was helped by the much greater reliance on markets that key economies in the region (e.g., China and Japan) decided to pursue and by the generally favorable environment for exports into other key markets, particularly the United States and other developed economies.

It is sometimes easy to turn a blind eye to the positive boost that progress toward freer and more open markets can give to economies. The debate on further market opening never stops. And negotiations on moving up the ladder toward freer and more open trade arrangements on the global scale can be tortuous and stretched. The Doha Round has continued to miss deadlines and, at the time of writing, it would appear to need heroic efforts to be brought back to life. Nonetheless, it is difficult to ignore the positive developments over the past decade in East Asia that have been facilitated by more open trading regimes.

More open trade regimes raise trade volume not only on the basis of factor endowments but increasingly also on the basis of economies of scale. Through the tight supply-chain management that new technology now makes possible, East Asia has made significant strides in intra-industry trade. Trade in parts and components has boosted intraregional trade, with various plants located in different countries being able to work in close sync with one another in order to more effectively and efficiently serve final consumer markets, particularly more developed markets such as the United States and the EU. Under supply-chain arrangements, specialized firms are being continuously pressed to innovate, improve quality, and cut costs as they try to take advantage of the increased size of the market they jointly serve. The combination of specialized focus and much larger volume gives greater impetus to further innovation.

Innovation used to be a near monopoly of the West, and East Asian firms had the reputation of being merely good copiers, cheap imitators, and technology pirates. In the past decade, however, as the relationship between production sites and final markets has become much closer and as supply chains have become more efficient, research and development networks have grown stronger and multiplied. Ideas have traveled more quickly and freely, and more innovation has occurred much closer to production sites in East Asia. The number of patents taken out by individuals and institutions in Northeast Asia—particularly in Japan, China, South Korea, and Taiwan—has gone up dramatically in recent years. The more open transmission of skills and the greater exchange of ideas and scientific insights have also been facilitated by easier and more frequent travel and by longer stays abroad on the part of research personnel from East Asia.

Where trade and technology lead, there finance follows. As real economic growth picked up and as the region's trade volume rose even more impressively, investment opportunities in the region became more attractive. China in particular, and to a lesser extent the other economies in East Asia, became the destination of FDI flows. In fact, every East Asian economy has taken advantage of higher FDI inflows and higher trade surpluses to build up their foreign exchange reserves. They also started to engage in initial conversations to set up at least limited arrangements through which to jointly mitigate financial risk. Through the Chiang Mai Initiative, economies in the region decided to set up a limited pool of exchange reserves as a first step toward ensuring against the return of the financial crisis of the 1990s. They also began discussion of an Asian bond market, and in 2002 the Asian Bond Markets Initiative was launched under ASEAN+3. All these are just slightly more than straws in the wind for now. But they point to the direction where winds will be blowing in the future, and that is toward greater regional financial cooperation.

Trade, technology, and finance have thus reinforced each other in a manner that has more broadly integrated East Asian economies with the global economy. In the process, they have also become much more closely integrated with each other, so that, substantively speaking, an East Asian economic region has emerged. The main pillars of this economic region are the big economies, Japan and China. Both have maintained largely open trade regimes. They also have relied more on the dynamics of market forces to drive the economic reforms they have been undertaking and, particularly in the case of China, to rev up their economic and export engines. The smaller economies in the region have pursued a similar market orientation and more open trade regimes. They too have contributed dynamically to the increasing integration of East Asia into the global economy, as well as to the emergence of the East Asian economic region.

As the East Asian economies have become increasingly integrated with the global economy mainly through greater reliance on market processes, they have increasingly been faced with challenges to their internal integration in the face of domestic disparities in economic opportunity and income. The economies of scale that trade, technology, and finance have made possible also have had consequences that put increasing pressure on the domestic cohesion of several East Asian societies.

Perhaps the most noticeable consequence is the increasing concentration of people and economic activity in cities. Increased economic activity tends to be location specific, and it tends to be concentrated in a few centers. Indeed, economies of scale call for concentration and even further agglomeration of economic activity and of people. People generally migrate from the less developed countryside, which has much fewer economic opportunities, to the centers of industrial production, trade, and export activity.

All this tends to widen the inequality of economic opportunity and income levels. The urban-rural divide widens, and gaps also grow between geographical segments of a nation's population (e.g., between south and north, east and west, or interior and coastal areas). Furthermore, the pressure of immigration into a few industrial urban centers brings spatial challenges such as congestion, garbage and sewage disposal, pollution, snarled traffic, and—where city governments are relatively weak—slums and squatter colonies as well. When all these challenges are not properly and adequately met, crime surges and the sense of security in urban areas deteriorates considerably.

The burden of having to meet these challenges falls on city governments, which have been required to adjust their governance paradigms and improve their technical capacity at a faster pace than normally expected. As challenges grow, so too do opportunities, as new and greater resources flood into these areas. Together with these opportunities comes greater temptation for graft and corruption on a large scale. For some ordinary city government officials, temptations are often too great to resist, so corruption quickly becomes a top priority as a public concern.

East Asia in the past decade has had to face these consequences, which challenge the internal, domestic cohesion of their societies. They have become increasingly serious concerns, and they keep crying out louder for more attention and purposeful action. The failure in some instances to meet these challenges has often given a bad face to globalization. Even in the societies of East Asia that have been benefiting from closer integration with the global economy, the word "globalization" itself often attracts the ire of demonstrators who are sufficiently incensed by the "triple Cs" that have come in the wake of economies of scale: cohesion, congestion, and corruption.

As East Asia moves forward toward becoming one economic region, the key issue that has to be resolved is how to continue to take advantage of the positive consequences of economies of scale while effectively confronting their negative consequences. In other words, how can East Asia continue to become more interconnected internally and with the rest of the world—i.e., continue with *global integration*—while resolving the difficult problems associated with cohesion, congestion, and corruption that are putting enormous pressure on the *domestic integration* of many societies in the region?

It is the need to face up to this issue that has opened many avenues for East Asia to move forward, beyond being merely one economic region to becoming more than an economic region, if not a community, in the decade ahead.

THE ROAD AHEAD FOR EAST ASIA

If East Asia has been able to post a remarkable recovery from the Asian financial crisis of a decade ago with heavy reliance on market-driven forces and more open trade regimes, then moving forward should draw impetus from the region's continued commitment to allowing markets to work. It would be foolhardy for the economies in the region to scale down on such a commitment, which can continue to provide tailwinds to their economic sails. Three areas in particular—trade, innovation, and finance—provide rich and fertile ground for the region to make further progress.

Either individually or through regional arrangements such as ASEAN+3, or more fittingly under the newer and broader auspices of the East Asia Summit, the economies in the region should continue to exploit economies of scale by facilitating the further growth and development of networks engaged in the parts and components trade. Indeed, there is wide scope for further expanding the regional production networks by broadening and further integrating the logistical supply-chain systems that already span several economies in the region. Intergovernmental initiatives could aim at simplifying, making consistent, and eventually unifying the wide variety of rules, such as those related to rules of origin, and more broadly the special economic partnership arrangements or bilateral trade agreements that have been and are in the process of being forged within East Asia.

Meanwhile, as innovation centers gain further ground and achieve more success within the region, more open mechanisms should be set up to ensure and enhance regional knowledge and technology spillovers. The flow of knowledge and technology should be expanded from the vertical channels running from the more developed economies outside the region, such as the United States and the EU, to the economies in Northeast Asia. This should be increasingly complemented by horizontal channels established between several of the economies in the region. To begin setting up these alternative horizontal channels and to systematically develop them, governments in the region should encourage and facilitate cooperation between research centers, scientific laboratories, and graduate institutes, including eventually between universities in the region. In the next few decades, regional cooperation should therefore include among its top priorities greater coordination and support for upgrading postsecondary education and creating more meaningful exchange programs, as well as for scientific and technical interaction between research institutes and graduate centers in various economies in the region.

Regional financial cooperation also needs to be pushed further. Now that the symbolic agreements to pool limited amounts of exchange reserves have been forged with the Chiang Mai Initiative, more substantive steps should be taken to expand on this. These may include the wider spread of improved risk management systems and the possible sharing of best practices in risk management at both the microeconomic and macroeconomic levels. Corporate bond markets need to be given further impetus so that financial markets can be further developed and strengthened in various economies. The initial efforts to link the region's capital markets more closely and more interactively should not be allowed to flag. The region's resolve to undertake these efforts should, instead, be strengthened by the stark imbalances—and the problems those imbalances create—in the financial relations between the individual economies in the region (e.g., China) and the more developed financial markets—particularly the US financial market.

The market trinity of trade, innovation, and finance, therefore, does provide rich and fertile ground for further economic growth and forward movement for the economies of the region. As they continue to work on this favorable ground, they need to consider undertaking further initiatives, such as those indicated in very broad terms above, either individually or preferably in solidarity with many other market-minded economies in the region. As they attempt to do so, they will find that they continue to rely mainly on governmental leadership and intergovernmental cooperation.

But the role of governments—i.e., the role of the state—in regional efforts needs to be increasingly complemented by the role of business enterprises and postsecondary educational institutions, such as universities and graduate research centers. Corporations and universities in the region need to be drawn much more proactively into the effort to address the challenges—there are always new and greater numbers of challenges—that market-oriented economies face. Moreover, these challenges arise from the dynamics of more open and robust competition within markets. And it is corporations, with postsecondary educational institutions playing a positive and supportive role, that need to meet the challenges of market competition. Beyond a certain point, after the "rules of the game" have been set and the framework for competition policy has been provided by governments and intergovernmental agreements, it is corporations, as organizations that stand or fall on the basis of their competitiveness and their general ability to maneuver effectively in the face of market forces, that should carry the ball. At that point and beyond, states should play less and less of a role within the economy, and corporations should take on more and more strategic and operational responsibility. In the decade ahead, East Asia may well be reaching this point.

If East Asia is to enter that stage in the next decade, and if business corporations are to play a much greater role on their own, with much less dependence on the state and state-managed arrangements, then the manner in which corporations are governed becomes a critical concern. The corporate governance of businesses that compete in increasingly free and open markets needs to be subject to clear "rules of the game" and a publicly accepted framework. Markets are increasingly demanding that these rules and this framework should be in line with professional and ethical standards as well as with the demands of social responsibility. Governments should insist on setting these rules and standards and on ensuring that the demands of social responsibility are met. But compliance remains the responsibility of the corporations themselves, which should increasingly hold themselves more transparently accountable to free and open markets. In living up to professional, technical, ethical, and social responsibility standards, corporations should be able to bank on the active and dynamic support of independent postsecondary educational institutions with their various graduate research centers and technical institutes.

Business corporations and postsecondary educational institutions operate at the microeconomic level within the macroeconomic "rules of the game" and market competition framework that governments provide. In the next few decades, the economies in East Asia will continue to rely on their governments to further improve the rules of the game and to enter into intergovernmental regional arrangements that further refine and operationalize the market competition framework for the region. More macroeconomic work needs to be undertaken and accomplished. But even more work at the microeconomic level needs to be accomplished so as to complement and give further substance to the work of and between governments in the region. Institution building in the corporate sector and at the level of specialized postsecondary educational and research institutes becomes even more compelling and important when viewed as a complement to continued nation building. Success in East Asia with regard to the former (institution building) as a major complement to the latter (further nation building) could help secure the further progress of East Asia as something more than an economically integrated region. Moreover, it would be a decisive step toward the loftier and more ambitious dream of becoming an East Asia community.

These steps, to be taken within the rich ground marked out by the market trinity of trade, innovation, and finance, need to be complemented by steps addressing the triple challenges that have come along with economic growth and high export volumes in the past decade—congestion, cohesion, and corruption. These need to be faced decisively and effectively, since the failure to address them properly could slow and eventually stall the economic and export engines of the region.

Megacities have developed and metropolitan centers have spread in the region, making the problem of congestion acute.[3] Fortunately, the development and spread of these megacities and metropolitan centers have been accompanied by the growth of many more mid-sized and small cities. Some of the congestion can be alleviated by providing more efficient connections between megacities or metropolitan centers and the emerging mid-sized and smaller cities. Resources are increasingly available, in part as a consequence of higher economic growth, from within the economies of East Asia for constructing the necessary infrastructure, such as roads, railways, airports, and harbors. Moreover, standards of public governance, even for mid-sized and small cities, are being raised. And greater efforts should be directed in the next decade toward sharing best practices in the public governance of cities and of the component cities and municipalities of metropolitan centers. More attention should be paid to closer coordination between governance initiatives of various local governments—and between the public works and infrastructure projects embedded in those initiatives—so that economies of scale can be positively tapped for greater interconnection between them. The external economies resulting from more efficient interconnections between cities and surrounding municipalities should be tapped to help address urban congestion and to make cities both more livable and more economically competitive.

The challenge to cohesion from rising inequality—brought in part by high economic and export growth in a few industrial centers—needs to be met by providing wider access to skills training, continuing education, and other social services, such as basic health care, as well as by mobilizing communities. To varying degrees, this access is already being provided through various programs that governments and civil society organizations (CSOs) are undertaking. Governments are finding, however, that there are limits to their effectiveness, particularly their cost-effectiveness, in providing such access to the much wider range of the population that such programs need to cover. CSOs, for their part, are also finding that they are subject to deficits of accountability and transparency. Moreover, the limited resources for—and the even more limited coordination between—their social outreach programs generally limit their overall effectiveness. Clearly, a greater exchange of best

---

3. A megacity is generally defined as an urban area with a population over 10 million. There are currently 25 megacities worldwide, and roughly one-third of these are in East Asia.

practices within economies as well as between economics in the region should be placed as a priority item on the regional cooperation agenda of East Asia. In particular, the exchange of best practices in providing access to various social services, and particularly access to skills formation and continuing education for those segments of the population unable to go on to postsecondary education, should be facilitated between the various economies in the region.

The challenge from corruption cannot be fully met by a simple decentralization of governmental power. Decentralization has to be accompanied by positive efforts to help local governments raise the standards of their public governance practices, starting with those responsible for mid-sized and smaller cities. Raising these standards requires more effective mechanisms for ensuring greater transparency and public accountability, and these mechanisms need to be systemic, involving the participation of the socially responsible sectors in the city. Often, a multisectoral coalition made up of business, academe, media, CSOs, and professional organizations can be encouraged to work positively and constructively with local officials of the city to pursue a common roadmap for the community. The public governance paradigm would call for their participation in and contribution to the accomplishment of various projects and targets embedded in the city roadmap. Thus, responsible citizens and public officials would have a joint stake in promoting the development of their city in a more transparent environment, with shared accountability and zero tolerance for corruption.

Indeed, throughout the region, political power is becoming more contestable. In many of the region's economies, a transition from the rule of man to the rule of law is well underway. As this transition gathers momentum, public governance initiatives aimed at raising transparency, accountability, and the standards of professionalism and social responsibility can be more openly shared. The emerging best practices, which have already been tested in a number of cities and local government units, should be more freely exchanged and more broadly spread across the region.

The triple challenges across the region from congestion; rising inequality straining internal, domestic cohesion; and corruption can be met in the next decade with the heavy involvement of governments. Not only national governments, however, need to be involved. Increasingly, local governments must also be given a greater share of the responsibility. These local governments, however, need to have their capacity for public governance brought up to higher levels of transparency, accountability, and professionalism. Also, at the local level, there is greater imperative, as well as greater opportunity, for the involvement and participation of various sectors and citizens groups. Provided they are steeped in the discipline of responsible citizenship, these groups can and should be brought into the public governance process as positive and meaningful contributors to good governance and community development. In light of this, the sharing of best practices in public governance, particularly at the local level, offers a rich field for regional cooperation in East Asia.

PROSPECTS FOR GREATER SOLIDARITY IN THE REGION

Moving forward, the agenda for the region is extremely broad, including initiatives that can be undertaken individually, within the economies in East Asia, as well as initiatives to be undertaken through greater regional cooperation. It spans a wide range, from initiatives building on the strengths already achieved through commitment to greater reliance on open and competitive markets to those addressing the weaknesses that have put heavy pressures on domestic cohesion and that have come largely in the wake of greater integration with global markets. The expansion of the agenda comes from the wider and deeper realization that East Asia has recovered from the financial crisis of a decade ago, and that it has done so by following a framework relying heavily on economies of scale and the imperative of maintaining domestic cohesion through higher standards of public governance practice.

Indeed, there is fertile ground for positive initiatives that draw impetus from the continued and even deeper commitment to market competition on the part of economies in East Asia. These initiatives would aim to improve the conditions in which the market trinity of trade, innovation, and finance can flourish. All these would require the continued involvement of national governments dealing with macroeconomic issues. But even greater involvement will be necessary on the part of business, supported by postsecondary research and educational institutions. Their involvement, necessarily more at the microeconomic level, must be guided by the principles and best practices of corporate and institutional governance in line with the professional and ethical standards that markets increasingly demand.

There is equally fertile ground for initiatives responding to the pressures exerted on domestic cohesion arising in part from higher economic and export growth in many parts of the region. Indeed, the pressures associated with the "triple Cs"—congestion, rising inequality that threatens domestic cohesion, and corruption—would have to be mitigated by positive initiatives on the part of national governments in the region. However, in many economies, governments at the national level are finding it necessary, even increasingly essential, to count on greater and more socially responsible involvement by local governments and intermediate social groups, starting with associations, particularly those promoting the interests of families within the community, and other local community groups. But at the subnational, local level, the standards of public governance practices need to be significantly improved. Transparency and accountability, as well as greater professional and technical competence, need to be added to social responsibility in the public governance practices of local governments that, meanwhile, must bank on the participation and sustained involvement of intermediate groups in the community.

All these initiatives will benefit from, and in some instances are ripe for, greater and more intense cooperation between the economies in the region. Therefore, it is clear that, moving forward, the agenda for regional cooperation in East Asia extends to concerns that go beyond the narrow fields traditionally reserved for macroeconomics and finance. It includes related fields that are made essential by more open market competition between business corporations at the microeconomic level as well as more substantive cooperation and mutual support between research and graduate institutions. Issues related to economic geography, such as the rise of middle-sized cities that are increasingly interconnected with each other and particularly with the larger metropolitan centers, also need to be on the agenda. The priority list also includes issues related to welfare economics such as access to skills training, continuing education, and other vital social services, especially for the more marginalized segments of the population. And looming up as umbrella issues are those directly connected with corporate, institutional, and public governance.

By taking on such a broader agenda, the economies of East Asia can find many concrete steps they can take individually and, increasingly, together as a regional group. These steps can add many more facets to the economic region they have already built in the decade after the Asian financial crisis. Should they succeed in adding these facets, it is possible that a realistic foundation can be laid for the East Asian economic region to begin moving more decisively toward building the components of greater cooperation, which in time can be put together to form an East Asia community. The impact could also lend wind to the sails driving further economic growth, and could even lead to much higher levels of integration within the region.

6

The Strategic Rationale for East Asia Community Building

Hitoshi Tanaka with Adam P. Liff

No longer merely a buzzword around the water coolers of ASEAN headquarters in Jakarta, "East Asian regionalism" has attracted global interest and become the focus of serious dialogue thanks to the proliferation of ministerial conferences and multilateral dialogue throughout the 1990s and into the new millennium. Recent meetings of both ASEAN+3 and the East Asia Summit have made it clear that the establishment of an East Asia community is a common goal of member states. Statements from the East Asia Summit suggest an expanding conceptualization of regionalism to include joint efforts to combat the spread of infectious disease, energy security, and other issues.[1] This trend is a clear manifestation of the fundamental changes in attitudes toward community building that are taking place throughout East Asia.

Despite substantial progress in cooperation, perhaps best evidenced by the proliferation of free trade negotiations and agreements in recent years, the primary impetus for enhancing regionalism and East Asian integration remains largely economic and market driven. While

---

1. Such efforts, it should be noted, nevertheless remain in the preliminary stages. See, for example, the "Cebu Declaration on East Asian Energy Security" (January 15, 2007) and the "Chairman's Statement of the Second East Asia Summit" on the ASEAN Secretariat website (www.aseansec.org).

expanding economic cooperation is certainly a positive development and an integral part of the community-building process, an exclusive focus on the economic advantages of regional integration betrays an excessively insular mindset and delays the realization of a more comprehensive, cooperative, and enduring community.

The relative lack of substantive progress beyond the economic sphere thus far is itself a reflection of the numerous obstacles that such efforts will inevitably face. The absence of a common cultural and religious heritage, stark economic disparities, emerging confrontational nationalism, widespread domestic governance issues, past US opposition to stronger regional institutions, and both traditional and nontraditional security threats make it abundantly clear that the realization of an East Asia community will be no easy task. Faced with the need to overcome such monumental challenges, there is uncertainty among policymakers about how best to move forward. As a result, efforts to consolidate ties throughout the region have thus far lacked a unified conceptualization of what form the process of East Asia community building should actually take.

The fundamental aim of this chapter is to delineate the political rationale for expanding community-building efforts and to explore its two core components. The first component is what we refer to as the "virtuous cycle" that exists between economic growth and political liberalization, each of which can have a positive impact on the long-term stability of East Asia. Second, we examine the necessity for a rules-based (rather than values-based) approach of "inclusive multilateralism," which aims to address regional issues through voluntary and coordinated actions, rather than allowing the most powerful governments in the region to govern by fiat. We argue that in light of contemporary realities in East Asia, an "*action-oriented regionalism*," a process through which states are bound together by rules and operations to proactively tackle functional issues of common concern, is the necessary starting point for this effort. Such an approach is the most practical way to deepen trust between states and gradually lay the groundwork for more substantive community building in the future.

While acknowledging that regionalization efforts should maintain the creation of a formalized "East Asia community" as the ultimate objective, we nevertheless hold that the true value of this pursuit lies not so much in the establishment of a European-style regional superstructure as in the *process* of community building itself. Given the current circumstances in the region, and in particular its vast diversity, a rules-based and process-oriented approach is the only practical strategy to gradually transcend existing obstacles and further consolidate the peace, prosperity, and stability of East Asia.

The Current Circumstances in East Asia

Before continuing on to a more in-depth discussion of the political rationale for the development of an East Asia community, it is necessary to first offer a brief summary of the current circumstances in the region.

The East Asia that exists today is vastly different from that of only a decade ago. Discourse on the region is now dominated by talk of the rise of China and India, two nations whose economies are on course to become the second and fourth largest in the world respectively within only two decades. Goldman Sachs, the global investment banking firm, predicts that China will continue on to pass the United States by 2035, with India following suit a mere ten years later.[2] The smaller developing economies are also growing at a torrid pace, with average gross domestic product (GDP) growth rates in the region passing 8 percent in 2006.[3] One need only look to the recent proliferation of bilateral and multilateral free trade agreements, soaring intraregional trade levels—currently surpassed only by those of the European Union (EU)-15[4]—and widespread governmental support for the expansion of Asian bond markets for ample evidence that regional economic integration is well underway. However, far from being limited to economic growth, the region's transformation is also increasingly noteworthy for the slow but steady shift toward a general embrace of democratic values. This development is manifest in the recent decisions of several formerly authoritarian governments to dramatically liberalize their political systems.

Within China, continued economic growth and the increasing prominence of domestic governance issues (e.g., tensions between economic

2. "India Projected to Join China in Surpassing the Size of the US Economy by 2050," *International Herald Tribune*, January 24, 2007.

3. Asian Development Bank (ADB), *Asia Development Outlook 2007* (Hong Kong: ADB, 2007).

4. Based on 2005 data, the level of intraregional trade has already reached 55 percent, a rate higher than the North American Free Trade Agreement, at 45 percent, and quickly approaching the 60 percent level of the EU. See Masahiro Kawai, "Toward a Regional Exchange Rate Regime in East Asia," ADB Institute Discussion Paper 68 (June 2007).

freedom and political freedom, widening income disparities, energy, and environmental issues) serve in many ways as a reflection of the challenges facing the region as a whole. Given its vast size, not only in terms of population but also economic influence, land area, and resource consumption, the rise of China is arguably the most significant global development in recent memory. China has been pursuing a benign yet increasingly assertive foreign policy, characterized by substantial and nontransparent annual increases in military spending and elements of nationalistic tendencies in conjunction with the 2008 Olympics in Beijing and the 2010 World Expo in Shanghai. This has sent policymakers in neighboring countries scrambling for effective means to hedge against the uncertainty surrounding its future path.

India's economy is also rapidly expanding. Historically one of the founding members of the Non-aligned Movement during the Cold War, India has in recent years gradually strengthened its ties with the West. In light of concerns surrounding China's rise, some Western policymakers hope to see India emerge as a collaborative partner on the global stage and as a potential balancer to China. This logic is clearly manifest in the nuclear cooperation deal between the United States and India, as well as in Australia's lifting of a decades-old ban on uranium sales to states that are non-signatories to the Nonproliferation Treaty. Engagement of India is by no means limited to the West, however. The ultimately successful campaign to include India as a member state in the East Asia Summit and former Japanese Prime Minister Shinzo Abe's rhetoric about the importance of enhancing "democratic partnerships" in the region are just two examples of similar movements occurring within East Asia.

One other evolution of note in the region is the gradual transformation of Japan. The primary change of relevance here is its growing assertiveness in international affairs, which is itself a reflection of structural changes in domestic politics, the economy, and the social fabric of Japanese society. Developments outside its borders have also played an important role in facilitating this assertiveness. For one, China's growing regional and global political influence has inflamed existing bilateral tensions and exacerbated competition for regional leadership. Additionally, the situation on the Korean Peninsula, in particular North Korea's October 2006 nuclear test and the continued controversy over its abduction of Japanese citizens, has also had a profound impact on Japanese public opinion. Concomitant with these trends and with a gradual decrease in domestic opposition, Japan's security policy is undergoing a significant transformation in the new century as it seeks a more proactive and "normal" role.

Turning our focus southward we find that, despite the substantial progress ASEAN has made in recent years, many of its members continue to struggle for better governance. While the region is certainly an economic success story, having posted annual GDP growth rates of over 5 percent for several years, corruption, environmental degradation, the absence of modern infrastructure, and an expanding gap between rich and poor nevertheless pose substantial threats to sustainable development. Although internecine warfare between ASEAN members has, with the exception of a few brief border skirmishes, largely become a relic of the past, nontraditional security threats such as maritime piracy, human and drug trafficking, and the spread of infectious disease remain issues of serious concern to both Southeast Asia and the greater region.

Toward an East Asia Community

Communities are groups that interact, have similar interests, and pursue a common destiny. While the number of leaders who have come out in support of a shared vision for the region has grown significantly in recent years, the obstacles that efforts to create an East Asia community will inevitably face in a region as diverse as East Asia remain substantial. In light of this reality, for the foreseeable future leaders are advised to focus their efforts not on the creation of a formalized "East Asia community" but on the process of community building itself.[5]

The Link between Economic Growth and Political Stability

As Jesus Estanislao effectively argues in Chapter 5, the economic rationale for increased interdependence within East Asia is quite clear.

---

5. Although the phrases "East Asia community" and "community building" have entered into common usage, the term "community" is perhaps too laden with connotations to accurately capture what is happening in East Asia. Bilahari Kausikan, for one, has suggested that a neutral term such as "architecture" might actually be more appropriate. Kausikan, "Constructing East Asia" (opening address, 5th Annual NEAT Conference, Singapore, August 21, 2007).

While there is no doubt that this consolidation of economic and financial ties is an absolutely integral part of the community-building process, these links should be treated as necessary but by themselves insufficient aspects of a larger process. Henceforth, regional leaders must give increased attention to the political benefits of prosperity and economic interdependence.

What exactly are the political benefits of expanding economic ties throughout East Asia? If economic community building expands to include trade in goods and services, investment, standards, and the movement of people, this would effectively set the stage for a regionwide economic partnership agreement, which in turn could develop into a broader Asia Pacific/APEC free trade zone. The gradual emergence of this kind of community, which should observe the rules and obligations of the global system and be linked to such international institutions as the World Trade Organization (WTO), would not only make the region more prosperous but also encourage further economic and political liberalization.

The link between economic growth and political liberalization is well established. While increased prosperity is of course not the only factor involved in determining whether a country undergoes democratization, one need only look to the postwar experience of a state like South Korea for evidence of the connection and its applicability to nations in East Asia. If considered together with the substantial evidence suggesting that democratic states rarely, if ever, use war as a means to settle disputes with other democracies, the positive contributions that economic growth and political liberalization stand to make to long-term regional peace and stability become clear. Put simply, economic growth supports political liberalization, which in turn leads to a more prosperous, stable, and peaceful region.

Unfortunately, despite the peace dividend that could potentially emerge from a further proliferation of democratic values throughout the region, East Asian leaders rarely cite the positive effects of political liberalization as a rationale in support (or defense) of regionalism. This hesitancy probably has two main sources. First, there is concern that an excessive focus on political liberalization and democracy would ostracize some leaders who might view such efforts as a case of outsiders meddling in domestic politics and thus as a violation of state sovereignty. However, if articulated in a manner sensitive to these concerns, any negative impact should be minimal. A second reason may be concern about the domestic instability that could potentially emerge in the process of political reform. The transition from autocracy to democracy is rarely problem free. While it would be irresponsible to ignore this reality, on balance the benefits of political liberalization far outweigh the risks; a more stable peace in East Asia serves the interests of all peoples in the region.

There is one important caveat regarding the relationship between regional economic growth and political stability: what is good for individual states may not necessarily be good for the stability of the region as a whole. Although seemingly counterintuitive, when it comes to community building, economic growth in a given country can be a double-edged sword. If the gap between wealthy states such as Singapore and underdeveloped states such as the so-called CLMV nations (i.e., Cambodia, Lao PDR, Myanmar, and Vietnam, whose people live on an average income of only US$1.38 per day[6]) continues to expand, the implications for regionalism could be disastrous. Under such circumstances, an East Asia characterized by "winners and losers" could emerge, where calls for the further advancement of regionalism would fall on deaf ears. This development would only confirm long-held suspicions among some skeptics that "community building" is nothing more than an excuse for the region's wealthier states to freely pursue their respective national interests.

In order to avoid such an outcome, more affluent nations with interests in East Asia must begin the process of alleviating economic disparities through greater contributions to market expansion, institutional capacity building, and human development in the region's poorer nations. Increasing official development assistance (ODA) to develop modern infrastructure and placing a higher priority on the intellectual component of foreign aid are only two examples of such policy options. The former would not only yield direct benefits for individuals and local businesses within the recipient countries but could also serve as a critically important factor in attracting foreign direct investment, which would in turn further contribute to national development. With regard to the latter, the success of programs undertaken by Japan and other nations in Vietnam and Lao PDR have clearly demonstrated that intellectual ODA can go far toward helping nations learn how to help themselves.

---

6. Calculated using 2006 data from the IMF's April 2007 World Economic Outlook Database (www.imf.org/external/pubs/ft/weo/2007/01/data/index.aspx).

Unless the advanced economies do more to address the widening economic gaps between states in the region, facilitate the development of physical infrastructure, and foster economic growth in poorer nations, not only could community-building efforts in East Asia be put at risk, but the very stability of the region could be threatened. However, if rich countries actively expand their efforts to alleviate these economic disparities, both the poorer states and the region as a whole will benefit. Countries with healthy economies tend to have relatively stable governments. Domestic political stability in turn facilitates the development of more durable and harmonious diplomatic relations among neighboring countries. In short, expanding economic integration throughout the region should lead to a virtuous cycle of mutually reinforcing economic and political ties, a process that will in turn make a great contribution to the peace and stability of East Asia.

Inclusive Multilateralism

Without a doubt, the single most important factor in East Asia's recent transformation has been the rise of China. By almost every traditional measure of national power, be it economics, politics, or the military, Chinese leaders aim to see their country achieve great power status in the near future. While China's emergence does not necessarily pose a direct threat to regional stability, it has nevertheless given rise to a great deal of apprehension throughout the region. To address these concerns and ensure that China becomes a responsible player in global affairs, it is abundantly clear that a return to a Cold War–era strategy of containment to preempt China's rise is not a realistic option. Not only would such a strategy play into the hands of hardliners within the PRC who call for China to adopt a more assertive and confrontational foreign policy, it would also reverse many of the positive effects of China's rise in the region, and in particular the valuable contribution it has made to global economic growth. Instead, a policy of cautious engagement that addresses, but does not fall victim to, the uncertainty and skepticism surrounding China's rise would be much more sensible.

This cautious engagement strategy would utilize two main approaches to achieve its goal of bringing China into the global community as a peaceful and responsible player. The first approach, which is beyond the scope of this chapter, consists of developing a kind of soft but firm hedge against the unpredictability of China's future course that at the same time takes care to avoid threatening or antagonizing its leaders. Briefly, this approach would most likely include a consolidation of strategic links among Japan, India, Australia, South Korea, and the United States, as well as a continued emphasis on US bilateral security alliances and partnerships in the region. The second approach is designed to engage both China and the rest of the region in "inclusive multilateralism," the goals of which are to gradually facilitate the proliferation of international norms throughout the region and to use multilateral dialogue and a significantly expanded emphasis on proactive and cooperative action to address issues of common concern. In the long run, these efforts will strengthen intraregional ties and engender relationships based on confidence, trust, and ultimately a shared sense of community.

Norm Proliferation

The expanding economic interdependence emerging in East Asia in recent years has made it so that sustainable cooperation is in the interest of each and every state. Institutions such as ASEAN+3, the ASEAN Regional Forum (ARF), and the recently established East Asia Summit demonstrate that regional leaders have come to believe in the benefits of cooperation and increasingly share a common vision for the region's future. These intergovernmental links, complemented by the rapid expansion of multinational corporations and the ongoing proliferation of various other transnational networks at all levels of society, have effectively laid the groundwork for the further expansion of multilateralism.

One of the primary mechanisms driving these developments has been the recent spread of international norms throughout the region. One need only look at the vast literature of international political and economic theory to find scholarship arguing that the spread of norms, rules, and international institutions is immensely beneficial for global peace and prosperity. While there remains a great deal of skepticism in some East Asian circles about the legitimacy of such claims, particularly in light of the trauma of the 1997 financial crisis, there is no doubt that the liberal norms of transparency and participation in rules-based institutions are gradually taking root in the region. Far from being exclusionary or particular to a (relatively) homogenous system like that of the EU, one need look no further than China's entry into the WTO for evidence that even countries that have yet to experience extensive domestic political liberalization can actively participate in and benefit from this kind of open and rules-based system. In fact, it is exactly this openness that has been the basis for much of the region's economic expansion in recent years.

While participation in these multilateral institutions is important in and of itself, what is of arguably still greater significance in the context of community building is the positive influence that these institutions can have on member states. Through participation in rules-based communities, nations gradually become "socialized" to realize the benefits of adopting certain modes of behavior. These norms are gradually internalized and, with time, are institutionalized, by which point the costs of attempting to "go against the grain" become so large that continued compliance is in every state's interest. In essence, despite the diversity of East Asia, if states come to adopt standardized rules and norms of behavior, such as increased transparency, the transaction costs of interaction will decrease. This process will in turn cultivate greater trust, confidence, and interdependency.

An example of the contribution such an outcome could make to regional peace and stability may prove instructive. One of the most significant obstacles to the realization of an East Asia community has been the sharp rise of nationalistic sentiment in the region in recent years, particularly in China, South Korea, and Japan. Although pride in one's country poses no direct danger to regional stability in and of itself, the nationalistic sentiment of interest here, manifested in such incidents as the anti-Japanese demonstrations that spread throughout China in the spring of 2005, could conceivably develop into a strain of exclusive, confrontational nationalism. For example, it is not overwhelmingly difficult to imagine a scenario in which China and Japan, driven by suspicions that the other is intent on acquiring regional hegemony, engage in a debilitating arms race with the potential to deal serious damage to regional stability and the community-building process. However, such confrontational nationalism is neither inevitable nor irreversible.

Whenever one looks for the origins of nationalistic sentiment in Northeast Asia, be it anti-Japanese sentiment in China, anti-Japanese/Chinese sentiment in South Korea, or anti-Chinese/North Korean sentiment in Japan, the answer often lies at least partially in domestic politics.[7] Leaders in any number of political systems sometimes see the pursuit of a populist or nationalistic foreign policy as a means of garnering popular support. Although such tactics may succeed in reaping short-term gains for the party in power, they can have dangerous consequences in the long run. In contrast, the leaders of a nation that is a member of a community that has adopted a norm of seeking multilateral solutions to intraregional issues depend on their neighbors for help in addressing problems outside national borders. Since regional stability is central to the national interest, the state's leaders will show an increased sensitivity to views and expectations of community partners rather than depending solely on the popular support of domestic constituencies. As domestic constituencies come to see the benefits of a more constructive and cooperative foreign policy, popular opinion will become increasingly supportive. The end result would be a more rational (or, at the very least, less provocative) foreign policy and mutually beneficial (as opposed to zero-sum) calculations of national interest.

In short, as states become socialized to these norms of interaction, multilateralism may become a means to transcend national egoism and ambition and minimize the deleterious effects of traditional power politics. This process would reduce confrontational nationalistic sentiment and could potentially, one day in the distant future, render concerns about the emergence of a militarist or expansionist power in the region obsolete. Any process that is able to remove or at least partially attenuate these concerns, which arguably pose the single largest obstacle to community-building efforts, would make an invaluable contribution to long-term peace and stability in East Asia.

---

7. Two points should be stressed here. First, in all instances, our argument that confrontational nationalism is detrimental to regional stability is not tantamount to a dismissal of the grievances of the protestors themselves, many of which can be considered legitimate. Second, we also reject claims, particularly prevalent in Western circles, that the recent rise in nationalist sentiment has been orchestrated by the central governments of certain countries and is therefore, so the argument often goes, nothing more than a) a foreign policy tool to guilt or intimidate other nations into giving it what it wants, or b) a clever scheme to manipulate public opinion and shore up popular support for the regime in power.

Action-Oriented Regionalism and an East Asia Security Forum

There is no doubt that the continued participation of regional states in constructive bilateral and multilateral diplomatic fora, as well as the gradual adoption of common norms of behavior, would yield immense benefits for East Asia and should remain a long-term objective of community-building efforts. Nevertheless, it is important to reiterate the fact that circumstances in East Asia differ significantly from those in a region like Europe, where similar values such as democracy and the rule of law already had very strong roots at the time of the EU's establishment. In contrast, East Asia is—as many pundits who are cynical about community building are wont to point out—a region of considerable diversity, where the legacy of history looms large and the political relationship between its two greatest powers is at times characterized more by mistrust and suspicion than anything approaching common values. The expectation that East Asian states could put aside their differences overnight and adopt new values and norms of behavior in the name of "community" is far-fetched, to say the least. While recent joint statements such as the 2005 Kuala Lumpur Declaration are welcome developments, leaders must take care not to oversell such abstract concepts as an "East Asia community" until the prerequisite foundation is more firmly established. This process will necessarily take time.

Going forward, the most effective way to facilitate the strengthening of community will be a functional approach to proactively address issues around which the interests of all countries in the region converge. In particular, an emphasis on *action-oriented regionalism*, through which states are bound together by rules and operations, rather than (necessarily) values, religion, or political systems, stands to make a significant contribution to the community-building process. This approach would go beyond existing dialogue-based multilateral institutions and engage states in proactive and cooperative efforts to tackle challenges of common concern.

As noted previously, the region currently faces a number of threats to sustainable development. A greater effort must be made to convince regional leaders of the urgency of these threats and the necessity of working in concert to solve them. The bad news is that no country is immune to potential devastation if a disruptive event were to occur. Somewhat paradoxically, the good news (at least in the context of this chapter) is also that no country is immune to potential devastation if a disruptive event were to occur. The logic is simple: since all states would be affected, all states therefore have an interest in preventing, or at least minimizing, the damage.

One core area ripe for functional cooperation in the region is the field of security. While the ARF maintains an important function as a broad security dialogue forum effective for confidence building among its members, very little in the form of concrete cooperative action ever results from its meetings.[8] When it comes to putting an end to maritime piracy, terrorism, or other issues with the potential to seriously threaten regional stability, merely discussing the issue, while by no means absent of value, is nevertheless wholly ineffective for actually solving the problem. What the region needs is a regionwide security forum with a mandate to take specific and proactive action against such common threats.

It is important to stress that this security forum would at no time in the immediate future serve as an alternative to existing bilateral security alliances and partnerships with the United States, which serve as a guarantor of regional stability. Rather, for the time being its function should be complementary in nature. There is no doubt that Europe's evolution took place within the US security guarantee and could not have occurred without it. While the thought may be less than appealing to some leaders in the region, for at least the foreseeable future, the reality is that the same holds true for East Asia. Without US involvement, no regional security institution has a realistic chance of success. While the global strategic environment has undergone a substantial transformation in recent years such that most threats now come from nonstate actors, these traditional "hard" security alliances and partnerships with the United States remain necessary hedges against unpredictable future threats. In stark contrast to the situation as recently as the mid-1990s, these ties are now seen by most actors—even China—as fundamentally stabilizing for the region at large. Every effort must be made to keep the United States engaged in the region and make clear that all regional leaders welcome its continued involvement. At the same time, the United States has a responsibility to clarify and renew its commitment to the region. One way for Washington to do so would be to sign a Treaty of Amity and Cooperation and join the East Asia Summit.

---

8. In fact, there is only one instance of cooperative action in the ARF's 13-year history, a two-day joint maritime security exercise held in Singapore in January 2007.

While US security links in the region are absolutely necessary, they are no longer sufficient to provide the kind of stability necessary for East Asia's continued growth. Rather, they must be complemented by new and more inclusive multilateral institutions with a broader mandate. One example of this kind of institution is the Six-Party Talks framework, which has emerged as an effective subregional security dialogue forum tasked with the resolution of the North Korean nuclear issue. It is worth noting that such a multilateral security dialogue forum, which involves the five most powerful states in the region cooperating on a common security threat, was all but unimaginable only a decade ago. Even after the nuclear issue is settled, the framework can continue to serve as a subregional channel for confidence building among its members.

The ultimate goal, however, should be the establishment of an "East Asia Security Forum" composed of the East Asia Summit member states, and having the full participation of the United States once it has signed the Treaty of Amity and Cooperation. This forum would be used to cooperatively address nontraditional security issues such as energy security and the environment, infectious disease, maritime piracy, and counterterrorism. Distinct from other multilateral institutions in the region, an East Asia Security Forum would be operational in its orientation and combine dialogue with a mandate for proactive action. At least initially, this mandate would necessarily remain limited in its scope. However, as states become accustomed to working together and gradually build the foundations of trust necessary for larger operations, the mandate could expand to tackle such issues as the proliferation of weapons of mass destruction through cooperative action similar to the American-led Proliferation Security Initiative. Collaboration of this sort would not only work toward solving both traditional and nontraditional security threats but would also serve as an effective confidence-building measure and, with time, could minimize the level of threat that some states in the region continue to perceive from their neighbors.[9]

In sum, multilateralism and community building should not be thought of as a means to impose limits on individual state sovereignty. Rather, these processes should be looked at as instruments with which to address regional problems—problems that can only be solved through cooperative action. For the time being, this kind of functional

9. For more on the East Asia Security Forum proposal, including an explanation of its differences with the ARF, see Hitoshi Tanaka, "East Asia Community Building: Toward an 'East Asia Security Forum,'" *East Asia Insights* 2, no. 2 (April 2007).

approach is the most practical way to push the community-building process forward.

CONCLUSION

East Asia has undergone a substantial transformation in recent years. While the region as a whole continues to achieve rapid economic growth and growing economic and financial interdependence, very serious issues such as overwhelming disparities in per capita GDP, resource scarcity, terrorism, maritime piracy, infectious disease, and environmental degradation still remain and demand greater attention. Common values remain elusive due to the considerable political, social, and religious diversity of the region. The nuclear issue on the Korean Peninsula and potential conflict across the Taiwan Strait pose continuing threats to regional stability. These are all challenges that cannot be overcome by prosperity and economic interdependence alone.

In this chapter, we have delineated what we see as the basic political rationale for an East Asia community. It is our hope that policymakers will place greater emphasis on the benefits of economic and political liberalization, the positive impact of the spread of norms and rules-based institutions, and the valuable role that action-oriented regionalism, as embodied in such new institutions as an East Asia Security Forum, could play in engendering a more stable and cooperative atmosphere in the region. As states find themselves increasingly bound together by rules and operations, this inclusive process will also lay the groundwork for still deeper regionalization and, ultimately, the formalization of an East Asia community.

7

Human Security Cooperation as a Building Block for East Asia Community

RIZAL SUKMA

The process of building an East Asia community is well underway, despite the continuing debate over the nature and the feasibility of such an undertaking. This started in the aftermath of the Asian financial crisis with the convening of the ASEAN+3 process, which promised closer ties and cooperation between Southeast and Northeast Asian states. The idea for an East Asia community was clarified through the vision set out by the East Asia Vision Group (EAVG), which was endorsed by the leaders of the ASEAN+3 countries at their fifth summit, held in Brunei in November 2001. The idea received further encouragement in November 2002, when the East Asia Study Group (EASG), which was proposed by President Kim Dae-jung to assess the recommendations of the EAVG, endorsed many of the EAVG's proposals. More importantly, the East Asia community-building process appeared to have gained further momentum when the leaders of 16 countries—the ASEAN+3 countries together with Australia, India, and New Zealand—gathered in Kuala Lumpur in December 2005 for the inaugural East Asia Summit and declared that "the East Asia Summit could play a significant role in community building in [East Asia]."[1]

Despite the enthusiasm about the prospects for regional community building in East Asia, the eventual nature of this community and the way in which the process should proceed remain subject to debate. Some critics have even expressed doubts as to whether the idea can ever really take off and become a reality. This chapter is not intended to revisit the pros and cons of the debate; rather it seeks to explore how cooperation in East Asia can contribute to and facilitate the long-term project of regional community building.

More specifically, this chapter examines how cooperation in areas related to human security could facilitate East Asia's regional community-building process. Cooperation on human security can provide a new impetus for states in the region to work together in managing common problems, which in turn could strengthen the basis for the further institutionalization of cooperation. The institutionalization of human security cooperation among East Asian states—either through ASEAN+3 or the East Asia Summit—would contribute to international efforts at building global governance regimes in areas related to human security. However, within the context of the East Asia community-building process, there is still the need for *mainstreaming* human security concerns, *securitizing* the issues, and *institutionalizing* cooperation, particularly among civil society organizations (CSOs), epistemic communities, and governments.

HUMAN SECURITY AND THE EAST ASIA COMMUNITY-BUILDING PROJECT

The concept of human security is emphasized in the three guiding documents of the East Asia community-building process. The final report of the EAVG clearly stated that one of the goals of an East Asia community would be "to advance human security and wellbeing."[2] Echoing the EAVG Report, the EASG maintained that it "is of the opinion that East Asian countries should intensify consultation and cooperation on transnational

---

1. ASEAN, "Kuala Lumpur Declaration on the East Asia Summit" (Kuala Lumpur, December 14, 2005).
2. EAVG, "Towards an East Asian Community: Region of Peace, Prosperity and Progress" (November 2001).

issues that affect human security and regional stability."[3] Then, in the Kuala Lumpur Declaration on the East Asia Summit, issued in December 2005, leaders of the participating states also promised to foster "cooperation in uplifting the lives and wellbeing of our peoples." The emphasis on human security in these three documents clearly demonstrates the recognition on the part of states in the region of the importance of human security as an area of regional cooperation.

Human security, as understood within the East Asian context, could provide the basis for interstate cooperation and facilitate the regional community-building process. While some East Asian countries and analysts recognize the importance of both human needs and human rights as the twin core of human security, many regional states, however, still emphasize the "human needs" dimension of the concept. Despite the absence of a consensus on the meaning of human security, the emphasis on the protection of human beings from everything that threatens human life, such as water shortages, poverty, natural disasters, environmental degradation, and diseases, could provide the basis for cooperation among East Asian states.

The inclusion of human security cooperation in the regional community-building project is more than just rhetorical. It fits well with the daunting challenges facing any experiment in building a "community" in a region as diverse as East Asia. At the same time, it also reflects a deep awareness about the complexity of regional dynamics and the nature of East Asia as a region still in flux, in both an economic sense and a security sense. The inclusion of human security as one of the goals of regional community building also provides an important platform from which the limits of the regional community-building process can be addressed. In other words, human security cooperation would not be hampered by the numerous problems and constraints that have characterized the process of East Asia community building.

The most salient obstacle to East Asia community building has been the experience gap between Southeast and Northeast Asia in terms of regional institution building. Unlike Southeast Asia, Northeast Asia has been characterized by the absence of any regional institution comparable to ASEAN. Various proposals to create a formal multilateral institution in the region have not really gotten off the ground. As a subregion, Northeast Asia certainly has unique characteristics and is faced with its own set of political,

---

3. EASG, "Final Report of the East Asia Study Group" (November 2002).

economic, and security problems and challenges. Even though the countries in the region have in fact been engaged in a Track II dialogue process since 1993 through the Northeast Asia Cooperation Dialogue, the complexity of the region's problems has not yet permitted this forum to become the precursor for the establishment of a formal regional institution.[4]

Second, of all the reasons underlying the absence of a multilateral security institution in the region, the problem of trust and cooperation is of particular importance. Multilateral cooperation is difficult due to the presence of complex historical memories that still influence contemporary mutual perceptions among regional states. These historical memories clearly sustain the animosity and suspicion among the states in the region.[5] As a result, there is still an insufficient accumulation of trust among regional players, such as between Japan on the one hand and China, South Korea, and North Korea on the other, or between the two Koreas. However, the ASEAN experience shows that it is through cooperation that trust is built, not the other way around. In other words, cooperation—despite a lack of initial trust—can create trust over time. And, within the ASEAN context, the process of trust building has been made possible by the fact that cooperation—which led to trust building—was carried out within a multilateral institution.

The third challenge to East Asia–wide cooperation and community building is the nature of the region as a theater for an ongoing power shift among its major powers. The rise of China has led to uneasy relations among the major powers within the grouping, and especially between China and Japan. Indeed, the first East Asia Summit itself was already overshadowed by growing tension in Sino-Japanese bilateral relations. The current dynamics of the US-China-Japan triangular relationship clearly demonstrate the emergence of a new regional order in the Asia Pacific region. The relationship among these three major

---

4. For discussions on the constraints to the creation of a regional institution in Northeast Asia, see, among others, Frank Umbach, "The Future of Multilateralism in Asia," *IRI-Review* 9, no. 1 (Winter 2003/Spring 2004): 180; Jack Pritchard, "Beyond Six Party Talks: An Opportunity to Establish a Framework for Multilateral Cooperation in the North Pacific" (conference paper, NORPAC Hokkaido Conference for North Pacific Issues, October 7, 2004); Kongdan Oh, "Northeast Asia: Changes and the Potential for a Cooperative Future," *NIRA Policy Research* (January 2003); and Chung Ok-nim, "Solving the Security Puzzle in Northeast Asia: A Multilateral Security Regime," *CNAPS Working Paper* (September 1, 2000).
5. See Tsuneo Akaha, "Non-Traditional Security Issues in Northeast Asia and Prospects for International Cooperation" (conference paper, Thinking Outside the Security Box Conference, United Nations University Seminar, New York, March 15, 2002).

powers will continue to be a complex one. While the three countries are seeking to establish cooperative relations among themselves, the signs of emerging competition are also evident. China, clearly a rising power with its own interests, seems to see Japan and the United States as the two powers that might limit its regional preeminence. Japan is anxious about China's future policy direction, a feeling shared by some ASEAN countries. Meanwhile, the United States is clearly opposed to the rise of a new power that might pose a challenge to its regional pre-eminence. The uncertainties associated with this power shift will serve as a major challenge to the East Asia community-building process in the years to come.

The fourth challenge is the elusive role of ASEAN in managing and driving the East Asia community-building process. Despite the positive role played by ASEAN in promoting regional cooperation beyond Southeast Asia, there have been continuing doubts about the ability of ASEAN to function effectively as the "driving force" of the East Asia community-building process. For example, within the ASEAN Regional Forum (ARF), which is often seen as an extension of ASEAN's model of regional security,[6] ASEAN's leadership "can do little to promote security [because] Northeast Asia and not Southeast Asia is the locus of regional strategic tension."[7] ASEAN's emphasis on a gradual process and consensus building is also seen as a problem that could prevent meaningful regional cooperation. Moreover, as ASEAN itself is seen as having difficulties in addressing its own problems, its ability to play a role beyond Southeast Asia has therefore been questioned.[8]

Despite such challenges and constraints to cooperation, it would be misleading to claim that Northeast Asian states, and for that matter all of the East Asian nations, are immune to more institutionalized mechanisms for regional cooperation. There have been a number

---

6. See Michael Leifer, "The Extension of ASEAN's Model of Regional Security," in *Nation, Region, and Context*, ed. Coral Bell (Canberra: Australian National University, 1995), 73–90.

7. Robyn Lim, "The ASEAN Regional Forum: Building on Sand," *Contemporary Southeast Asia* 20, no. 2 (August 1998): 115.

8. For an analysis of ASEAN's problems since 1997, see Rizal Sukma, "The Declining Role of ASEAN as a Manager of Regional Order" (conference paper, NIDS Workshop on Regional Security Order in Asia, Tokyo, October 23–24, 2000); and Rizal Sukma, "Assessing ASEAN Vision 2020: The Political and Security Dimension" (conference paper, First ASEAN's People Assembly, Batam, Indonesia, November 24–26, 2000).

of opportunities for such an undertaking to succeed in the longer term. The most important opportunity for broader cooperation in East Asia has been presented by the capacity for ASEAN to play a pivotal role in extending its model of regional cooperation to the wider East Asian region. Despite its limitations, it was, and still is, the ASEAN-driven multilateralism that has paved the way for greater regional cooperation between countries in Southeast and Northeast Asia. In the aftermath of the 1997 financial crisis, ASEAN managed to reinvent and redefine its role as a "manager" of the regional order that would be acceptable to all major powers, thus making it possible for it to serve as a "hub" linking all of the East Asian states in a web of functional cooperation.

Second, ASEAN's management of cooperative interactions has helped build a growing habit of security dialogue (within the ARF) and cooperation (through the ASEAN+3 process) in the region. For its part, the ARF facilitates the regional learning process by providing a venue where every member state can become more comfortable with the idea and the merits of multilateral cooperation in the area of security. Such an undertaking, if sustained, will contribute to creating a habit of dialogue. As demonstrated in the 40-year experience of ASEAN, the institutionalization of a habit of dialogue and a culture of consultation contributed significantly to the institutionalization of an attitude of self-restraint and mutual respect among member states. Similarly, ASEAN+3 also helps create a habit of cooperation. This began modestly as an informal meeting among the foreign ministers of Southeast and Northeast Asian countries. The process, however, accelerated with the institutionalization of the ASEAN+3 Summit, which now provides a framework for cooperation not only between the ASEAN states and Japan, China, and South Korea but also among the three Northeast Asian states themselves.

Third, the emergence of common problems—especially the nontraditional security challenges that pose serious threats to human security—provides an opportunity for regional states to work together to address them. Both subregions—Southeast Asia and Northeast Asia—have recognized the threats posed by nontraditional security challenges to human security, and both have recognized the imperative of advocating and preserving human security as an essential element in the attainment of national security. In Northeast Asia itself, at least six major nontraditional security challenges can be identified: environmental degradation, resource scarcity, energy supply and distribution, migration, economic gaps, and illicit trafficking in drugs, weapons, and humans.[9] Similar problems are also shared by Southeast Asian countries. Therefore, East Asian countries, as well as Australia, India, and New Zealand, indeed share a common concern and agenda that should bind them together in a common endeavor to address these problems and to promote human security in the region.

The ability of East Asian states to overcome the problems of regional community building would be greatly strengthened if human security cooperation were to serve as the starting point during the formative years of the institution-building phase. For this purpose, it is imperative that human security be elevated to a higher priority in the regional community-building process. Such a focus would contribute not only to the creation of an East Asia community itself but also to international efforts to build global governance regimes in areas related to human security.

EAST ASIA'S GROWING RECEPTIVITY TO HUMAN SECURITY

Cooperation among East Asian states on human security has become more feasible due to the presence of a number of facilitating factors in the region. First, there is a growing domestic constituency for the promotion of human security in most East Asian states.[10] Human security approaches require collaboration among various sectors of society, and civil society—which has historically been one weak link in East Asia—has increasingly become an important player in promoting this agenda. The region has witnessed the emergence of nongovernmental organizations (NGOs) and other CSOs in various countries, including in China, that are beginning to address the problems of human security. Indeed, as "human security concentrates on justice and emancipation,"[11] the role of NGOs and other CSOs becomes an indispensable element in the process of ensuring and promoting human

---

9. See Tsuneo Akaha, "Non-Traditional Security Issues in Northeast Asia."
10. Paul M. Evans, "Human Security and East Asia: In the Beginning," *Journal of East Asian Studies* 4 (2004): 277–278.
11. Lee Shin-hwa, *Promoting Human Security: Ethical, Normative and Educational Frameworks in East Asia* (Seoul: Korean National Commission and UNESCO, 2004), 31.

security. In addition to serving as important societal forces that advocate and promote human security agendas within national boundaries, NGOs and CSOs "can be invaluable when it comes to coordinating and mounting the types of international operation[s] that the human security approach embraces."[12]

The recognition by East Asia's governments of the important role of NGOs and CSOs clearly provides a greater opportunity for regional cooperation. As the EAVG Report stresses, it is important for the governments in the region "to work closely with NGOs in policy consultation and coordination to encourage civic participation and responsibility and to promote state–civil society partnership in tackling social problems."[13] The EASG Report also called for the establishment of an East Asia Forum "consisting of the region's governmental and nongovernmental representatives from various sectors, with the aim to serve as an institutional mechanism for broad-based social exchanges and, ultimately, regional cooperation."[14]

Second, the prospects for institutionalizing the promotion of human security and deepening cooperation in this area are far greater now than before due to the changing conception of national security in the region. None of the East Asian states now sees security only in its narrow military sense. ASEAN, for example, has long championed the broad notion of security as encompassing both military and nonmilitary aspects, including the security of "the people." Japan and South Korea have been at the forefront in advocating and promoting human security approaches in the region and beyond. China, which was initially reluctant to embrace the concept, has also begun to see the value of defining security in this context, as reflected in its enunciation of the "New Security Concept." In other words, a human security approach is now more acceptable to states in the East Asia region. [15]

Third, there is also the effect of the institution building (through ASEAN, ASEAN+3, the ARF, and the East Asia Summit) that has already advanced in the East Asia region, which has helped give rise

---

12. Withaya Sucharithanarugse, "The Concept of 'Human Security' Extended: 'Asianizing' the Paradigm," in *Asia's Emerging Regional Order: Reconciling Traditional and Human Security*, ed. William T. Tow, Ramesh Thakur, and In-Taek Hyun (Tokyo: UNU, 2000), 59.
13. EAVG, "Towards an East Asian Community," 24.
14. EASG, "Final Report of the East Asia Study Group," 32.
15. For a discussion on the changing views of East Asian governments, see Evans, "Human Security and East Asia."

to a growing desire and commitment to institutionalize cooperation. As mentioned above, through their previous experience with various regional cooperation initiatives, states in East Asia have come to value multilateral cooperation as an important way to achieve peace and prosperity. The ASEAN+3 process, for example, has clearly emerged as an institutionalized vehicle for member states to cooperate in functional areas. More importantly, governments in the region have also benefited from regional cooperation to ensure the security of their people. The effective regional response in addressing severe acute respiratory syndrome (SARS), for example, clearly demonstrated the value of regional cooperation in the area of human security. Consequently, states in the region have become more comfortable with regional cooperation because of the ways in which it has enhanced their wellbeing.

Fourth, the prospects for greater cooperation in the area of human security have also been enhanced by the growing interdependence of states in the region. This, among other developments, has been perpetuated by the growing number of transnational threats to the security of individual states in the region. Within Southeast Asia, for example, problems such as human trafficking, marine pollution, infectious disease, haze, piracy, illegal logging, and transnational crime are all transboundary in nature and require greater regional efforts in combating them. Similarly, in Northeast Asia, as mentioned above, efforts to address the problems of environmental degradation, resource scarcity, energy supply and distribution, migration, economic gaps, and trafficking in drugs, weapons, and humans also require close coordination among regional states. None of these problems can be tackled effectively through unilateral action by individual states. In other words, the recognition by governments in the region of the interdependent nature of the problems they face could serve as an important facilitating factor for closer regional cooperation, which in turn can contribute to the regional community-building process.

Human Security Cooperation in East Asia: Prospects and Implications for Global Governance

The focus on human security would benefit not only the region; it also has significant implications for the capacity of global governance to address global problems. First, it would create and consolidate regional regimes for addressing and tackling global problems. The experience of the region in dealing with the problem of infectious disease is a case in point. For example, the ability of states in the region to cooperate closely among themselves and also with the World Health Organization in preventing the spread of SARS clearly helped in maintaining global health security. If human security cooperation could be further institutionalized within the East Asia community-building project, the efficacy of regional initiatives to address regional and global health problems would be greatly enhanced. The establishment of regional mechanisms to address human security problems would also facilitate greater international coordination in addressing and tackling problems with global implications such as climate change, water scarcity, natural disasters, and infectious diseases.

Second, from a strategic point of view, the East Asia community-building process could also serve as a mechanism for managing the regional and global implications of the power shift underway now in East Asia. As mentioned above, this process is still fluid, and its consequences for regional relations are still unpredictable.[16] This particular issue therefore requires careful management that regulates major power relations in the region. Competition among the major powers can be avoided if they see each other as partners rather than competitors. Indeed, the need to cooperate in promoting human security would make it imperative for states to see each other as partners instead of competitors. In other words, addressing human security problems, which require collaborative and joint efforts, clearly serves as an incentive to cooperate. And this incentive to cooperate would contribute to the reduction of incentives for the kind of competition among the major powers that would affect global security.

Third, regional cooperation in addressing human security concerns would strengthen existing global norms and rules. Two particular global norms are of paramount importance in this regard. First, as the problems facing the global community have increasingly become more complex, it is imperative for states to engage in global cooperation to overcome them. Cooperation, then, should become a norm, not an exception in contemporary international relations. Second, human

---

16. For an excellent discussion on the power shift and its possible consequences in East Asia, see David Shambaugh, ed., *Power Shift: China and Asia's New Dynamics* (Berkeley: University of California Press, 2005).

security cooperation in East Asia, regardless of the extent to which it can be carried out, would also contribute to the socialization of regional states and greater acceptance of "the responsibility to protect." To a degree, states engaging in human security cooperation are in effect also engaged in an exercise to advance the norm of the "responsibility to protect." However, it is important to note that the possibility for a greater acceptance of "the responsibility to protect" does not necessarily mean the abandonment of the principle of noninterference. Unless democracy becomes a common regional norm, the participation of East Asian states in undertaking "the responsibility to protect" would be carried out in a manner that would not compromise national sovereignty.

Indeed, the value of the East Asia community-building project does not lie only in the promotion of good interstate relations at the regional level. The project would also have positive implications for global governance. For East Asian states, especially in light of the challenges to regional community building discussed above, human security cooperation would serve as a more promising platform for increasing the incentives to cooperate. In other words, the success of the East Asia community-building project would, to a degree, depend on the institutionalization of habits of cooperation, which could be conveniently facilitated by pooling common resources to resolve human security problems in the region.

CONCLUSION: MAINSTREAMING, SECURITIZATION, AND INSTITUTIONALIZATION

For East Asia, cooperation on human security issues could provide a platform for developing the habit of cooperating within a formal multilateral setting. Within this setting, states could institutionalize the notion of "security with" rather than "security against" as the dominant paradigm for interstate relations. In the formative years, such multilateral cooperation should not concern itself excessively with results. Again, as ASEAN's experience has shown, the process is also important, especially for institutions to mature and to induce a level of comfort among the participating states. And, in the wider East Asia region, there are vast numbers of human security issues on which countries in the region could cooperate. The East Asia community-building project, therefore, should begin the process of institutionalization by focusing its agenda on cooperation in these areas first before it moves to traditional security areas.

However, the promotion of human security cooperation within the East Asia community-building project still requires a synergy of multiple strategies linking together governments, epistemic communities, and CSOs. This synergy requires the *mainstreaming* of human security concerns, the *securitizing* of the issues, and the *institutionalizing* of cooperation. First, a mainstreaming strategy is needed to further promote the human security agenda as an important element of multilateral cooperation in the region. There is always the risk that traditional security problems in East Asia, such as the territorial dispute between China and Japan and the problem of nuclear proliferation on the Korean Peninsula, might distract East Asian states from focusing on human security cooperation. More importantly, a focus on human security also requires the governments in the region to recognize the importance of bringing "the people" back to the center of the security discourse and practice. In this context, the mainstreaming of human security issues would be greatly facilitated by and requires the active role of CSOs and regional networks among them.

Second, the mainstreaming of human security concerns requires a degree of securitization of the issues.[17] Here again, governments can be easily distracted by the imperative to address traditional security problems, and in East Asia there is no shortage of such problems. Within the Northeast Asian context, the nuclear issue on the Korean Peninsula, the possible rivalry between China and Japan, the potentially unstable nature of Sino-US relations, and a number of unresolved territorial disputes continue to form core national security concerns for states in the region. Concerns about protecting human beings from threats no less deadly than war could be easily lost in the face of overriding concerns about traditional security. The primacy of state sovereignty also remains a major obstacle to human security cooperation. Within this context, human security issues need to be securitized so that they will attract more attention from governments. In this regard, the strategy of securitization requires the active role of the epistemic community, especially policy analysts. More importantly, the epistemic community can remind states to change their understanding of security "from an

---

17. For the meaning and strategy of securitization, see Ralf Emmers, "The Securitization of Transnational Crime in ASEAN," *IDSS Working Paper No. 39* (November 2002).

exclusive stress on territorial security to a much greater stress on people's security; and from security through armaments to security through sustainable development."[18]

Third, there is a need for the institutionalization of cooperation that requires the political will of governments. As mentioned earlier, regional cooperation in addressing human security problems is more effective if it is carried out within a multilateral setting. The imperative of institution-alization would take two forms. First, as most human security problems originate from within the domestic domain of states, it is absolutely critical for individual states to strengthen their national capacity to ad-dress these problems. Second, in order for human security responses to be effective, greater institutionalization of regional cooperation is required to build capacity at the national and regional levels to address human security threats. Southeast and Northeast Asian countries have made much progress in this area within the ASEAN+3 process. Now, it is time to broaden and deepen this undertaking within the wider East Asia community-building project, which involves Australia, New Zealand, and India, by taking up a focus on human security as a key item for the community-building agenda.

---

18. UNDP, "Human Development Report 1994," as reprinted in *Current History* (May 1995): 230.

IV

East Asian Regionalism in the International Community

8

US Perspectives on East Asia Community Building

FRANK JANNUZI

In the 40 years since the creation of ASEAN, the geopolitical landscape of East Asia has changed dramatically. The Cold War, with the divisions it exacerbated, has ended. States once governed by authoritarian regimes have developed into multiparty democracies. Bitter rivals have found, at least in some cases, that reconciliation and economic interdependence are far preferable to bellicose relations and economic self-reliance. Significantly, China has emerged as a major economic and military force, an aspiring great power whose explosive growth is reshaping the contours not only of East Asia but of the entire globe. Together, China and its great power neighbors—Japan and India—are eyeing each other warily, occasionally elbowing each other as they strive to secure their economic and security interests in the world's most dynamic region.

On the 40th anniversary of ASEAN, it is an appropriate time to take stock of the efforts of East Asian states to forge a cohesive community marked by common interests and effective multilateral organizations, and to discuss Washington's response to these efforts. Washington was an early proponent of an East Asia community when it sought to cobble together an Asian version of NATO to thwart Soviet and "Red Chinese" ambitions during the Cold War. But those efforts largely foundered, disrupted by nagging intraregional disputes and undermined by a latent

Asian antipathy for anything that reeked of European or Japanese (or American) colonialism. Steps toward regionalism were also hampered by squabbles over the very definition of East Asia, with some arguing for a narrow geographic understanding of East Asia as the nations of ASEAN plus China, Japan, and Korea, while others advocate a larger grouping adding India, Australia, and New Zealand. A still wider definition, embodied by APEC, embraces nations on both shores of the Pacific, including the United States.

In the absence of effective multilateral organizations in East Asia, the United States came to rely more on its bilateral alliances than on any regional grouping, to the point where by the mid-1990s Washington's attitude about East Asia community building had morphed from Cold War enthusiasm to something approaching post–Cold War disdain.

In the 1990s, the United States thwarted early steps toward building an East Asia economic community, fearing a diminution in US influence. More recently, however, the United States has awakened to the potential benefits (as well as the pitfalls) of a genuine East Asia community. As discussed below, this new interest in an East Asia community is the result of three developments: 1) the rise of China; 2) the emergence of transnational threats that call out for multinational remedies; and 3) an awareness that the nations of East Asia appear determined to forge an East Asia community, with or without the United States, and that US economic interests will be best served by promoting the creation of an East Asia community that is open to US trade and investment.

US attitudes toward East Asian regionalism are shifting incrementally. It now seems likely that Washington's initial responses to the changing strategic environment will include at least two elements: 1) redefining and reinvigorating its traditional bilateral alliances, using them as a bridge to secure vital US *security* interests until such time as a genuinely integrated and capable East Asia community emerges; and 2) negotiating a web of bilateral free trade agreements (FTAs) to secure US market access in anticipation of the *eventual* emergence of a regional free trade area built upon one of several competing foundations (ASEAN, ASEAN+3, ASEAN+6, or APEC). What remains unclear is whether the United States will embark on a third course of action—active support for building an East Asia community that will promote regional peace and security, foster economic integration, and nurture democratic governance and respect for human rights. If the United States wants to see the emergence of such a community, it will have to do more than sit on the sidelines. It will have to get in the game.

LUKEWARM ON REGIONALISM?

Any examination of US attitudes toward East Asian regionalism should begin with the disclaimer that the US government and American East Asia specialists are not of one mind on the issue. There are almost as many views on the subject as there are people studying it, and attitudes have shifted over time. A second caveat is that the US view of East Asian regionalism is not forged in isolation but rather in connection with the views of other players, especially China and Japan. These three nations are likely to ricochet off one another, with US enthusiasm for regionalism waxing and waning depending in part on whether China and Japan are judged to be supporting or opposing the creation of an East Asia community. Ironically, Chinese and Japanese enthusiasm for community building has sometimes contributed to US malaise, while Chinese and Japanese detachment has only led to US ennui. Finally, although efforts to build an East Asia community are very much on the minds of leaders in the region, it must be said that foreign policy officials in Washington in 2007 are more likely to be focused on the war in Iraq, instability in the Middle East, terrorism, and nuclear nonproliferation than they are on Asia's progress toward economic or political cohesion. A lack of sustained, high-level attention to East Asia policy tends to make US attitudes toward East Asian regionalism a moot point at the moment.

Still, it is possible to discern certain macro trends in US thinking on the subject of multilateralism in general and the building of an East Asia community in particular. During the Cold War, the United States recognized the utility, indeed the strategic *imperative*, of encouraging regional groupings that could balance Soviet influence and ultimately safeguard democratic systems and open markets. More often than not, the United States sought to be a formal member of these groups—as with NATO, the Organization of American States, and the Southeast Asia Treaty Organization—or at least an active observer—as with ASEAN, where the United States is both a "dialogue partner" and a participant in the ASEAN Regional Forum (ARF), created in 1994.

Toward the end of the Cold War, Washington had little time for a brand of East Asia regionalism that seemed to offer little in the way of strategic or economic value. ASEAN's timid response to the Tiananmen Square massacre seemed to illustrate for many in Washington the futility of attempting to forge an East Asia community that would champion cherished Western political values.[1] And yet, following the collapse of the Soviet Union, the geopolitical landscape of the world changed, as did Washington's perception of the role and value of multilateral organizations. With the end of the Cold War, Washington no longer looked to regional groups to alter the global balance of power. But this did not mean that regional organizations were without value. Rather, the United States began to work more actively with regional groupings to address transnational security threats or to promote regional peace and stability.

In East Asia, the end of the Cold War created new opportunities for collaboration among ASEAN states and between the members of ASEAN and neighboring great powers. The Paris Peace Accords of October 1991 marked the end of the Cambodian conflict and also set the stage for a new era of cooperation among former antagonists. Vietnam joined ASEAN in 1995, and China fully normalized relations with Vietnam, Indonesia, Malaysia, and the Philippines after years of tense relations. The end of the Cold War thus made possible new ad hoc partnerships in East Asia, but it also deprived ASEAN of one of its organizing principles—its opposition to Chinese- and Soviet-inspired communist movements in Southeast Asia.[2] When that common threat disappeared, many of the traditional rivalries among Southeast Asian states reemerged, sometimes making it difficult for ASEAN to reach consensus, and limiting ASEAN's value in the eyes of US policymakers.

With respect to hardcore national security interests, the end of the Cold War prompted the United States to reemphasize America's web of bilateral alliances in East Asia. In a *unipolar* world, the need to forge regional groupings as counterweights to competing great powers seemed

---

1. Washington has long held unrealistic expectations about the role that ASEAN, an organization founded on the principle of noninterference in the internal affairs of member states, might play as a champion of democracy and human rights in East Asia. Those unrealistic expectations continue today. The newly adopted ASEAN Charter ostensibly obligates member states to play a more active role in the promotion of human rights and the rule of law, but it nonetheless preserves ASEAN's respect for state sovereignty, even when a state's gross misconduct might reasonably justify outside involvement.
2. During the Cold War, China funded, trained, and equipped communist parties and communist insurgencies in every Southeast Asian state with the exceptions of Singapore and Brunei.

less urgent. And so, although ASEAN gained some limited currency as an organization capable of promoting intraregional political cooperation and economic integration, ASEAN was not judged by Washington to be a pillar of strength. To the contrary, Washington in the 1990s tended to shift its priority to bilateral partnerships focused on narrow, achievable results. The Clinton administration did not place much faith in multi-lateral organizations focused on broad, sometimes amorphous goals. Absent a strong domestic political push from Americans of Eastern European descent, even NATO expansion would probably have never occurred during this unipolar period. The United States still worked to promote regional economic blocks of its own design (e.g., the North American Free Trade Agreement, or NAFTA), but it generally frowned upon the formation of regional groupings that might exclude the United States or have the effect of diminishing US global influence.[3] This US tendency to rely on bilateral alliances reflects a deep-rooted American skepticism about the efficacy of regional or global governing institutions to address critical national challenges. In East Asia, the preference for bilateralism also reflects the dominant position of the US-Japan alliance and the perception that Japan—saddled with constitutional restrictions on collective self-defense—could not operate effectively within a NATO-style regional alliance structure.

9/11 WAKE-UP CALL

The United States got a painful reminder on September 11, 2001, that many emerging nontraditional security threats—not only terrorism wielded by extremist Islamic groups but also energy security, environ-mental degradation, pandemic influenza, and nuclear proliferation—were distinctly transnational in nature and called out for multilateral approaches. Information and technologies need to be shared, law enforcement efforts coordinated, and aid policies synchronized to meet these new challenges. From Washington's perspective, regional groups also seem desirable as a response to the emergence of China as a potential peer competitor and to the resurgence of North Korea's nuclear ambitions.

---

3. The Clinton administration was notably cool to the notion of an Asian Monetary Fund during the Asian financial crisis, and the United States has also taken a dim view of the Shanghai Cooperation Organization and the East Asia Summit.

Yet, as viewed from Washington, the capacity of multilateral organizations in East Asia remains quite modest, particularly when compared (as it inevitably is) with Europe, where alliance structures are robust and the process of community building is further along. There is no NATO in East Asia, and no OSCE [Organization for Security and Cooperation in Europe] reflecting a common commitment to developing effective democratic governance in weak states. To be sure, East Asian nations are adapting existing institutions and building new ones to enhance regional economic integration, promote good governance, and better address both traditional security concerns and transnational human security challenges, but these efforts are all still in their early stages. Will East Asia develop regionalism based on issue-oriented functionalism, or will the region resign itself to the more modest goal of trying to set norms? Can the nations of East Asia achieve even this second, more modest, objective?

The diversity of East Asia is one of its greatest strengths, but it also poses serious obstacles to effective multilateralism. The nations of the region have divergent interests and are in different stages of economic and political development, making it difficult to reach consensus and agree on concrete steps to address common challenges. Outside observers of East Asian regionalism often criticize ASEAN and its various appendages as "talk shops," lacking in substance.

Therefore, although the United States likes the *idea* of an East Asia community and has sometimes sought to play an active, constructive role in promoting regionalism, Washington will not bet its future on the ability of East Asian states to pull together an effective union with a common set of security objectives, economic policies, and a shared commitment to democratic governance and human rights. Washington strategists believe forging such a community will take years, and in the mean time, the United States, with its objective-driven foreign policy, will seek to preserve and strengthen its traditional bilateral alliances. These alliances represent a hedge against the uncertainties of China's rise, including the possibility that Beijing might come to dominate a more integrated East Asia community. Alliances, bolstered by bilateral FTAs, also allow the United States to hedge economically against the possibility that East Asian states might attempt to form a trading block that would disadvantage the United States.

To enhance the value of its traditional alliances and to make them more relevant to post–Cold War challenges, Washington has tried in recent years to make them less exclusive. As is discussed below, Washington is encouraging allies to work in concert with other state actors and emerging regional organizations based on common interests and values. The Proliferation Security Initiative (PSI) is one example of this, an effort to prevent the spread of weapons of mass destruction relying heavily, but not exclusively, on US allies. The Six-Party Talks are another example, pulling together two close US allies—South Korea and Japan—and forging an ad hoc group with two former rivals for power and influence in East Asia—China and Russia. Building on the platform provided by its alliances, the United States has led a diverse group of states sharing a common commitment to the goal of dismantling North Korea's nuclear program.

SKEPTICISM ABOUT REGIONAL GOVERNANCE AND MULTILATERAL INSTITUTIONS

Alliances are often thought to exist more as a *counterpart* or alternative to efforts at global governance than as a *complement* to those efforts. Many supporters of traditional alliances doubt the utility of multilateral institutions and all but the most robust multilateral alliances (i.e., NATO). In fact, attempts to advance global peace and security by negotiating new treaties, developing new international norms, or building new networks of nations or multilateral institutions have been roundly criticized by scholars who doubt the very existence of international law.

These critics question the efficacy of any organization that is not backed by a sovereign state wielding the threat of force. They place little stock in the World Trade Organization (WTO) or the UN, much less APEC, the ARF, East Asia community, or other multilateral organizations. They have little confidence that an anarchic world can be brought into line by toothless treaties such as the Treaty of Amity and Cooperation or by consensus-based multilateral organizations such as ASEAN. They point to the failure of the Kyoto Protocol as a case in point, with even Japan, the host of the talks, failing miserably to meet its Kyoto emissions targets. These skeptics—they would call themselves realists— look with dismay at Burma, a country that has stubbornly resisted lackluster efforts by ASEAN and the UN to promote civilian rule and the release of opposition political figure and Nobel Laureate Aung

San Suu Kyi. Finally, they wonder how any East Asia community could provide an effective counterbalance to China's growing dominance in the region, worrying that China would use its influence to bend any regional group to its will by exploiting the differences among its neighbors.

Former US Ambassador to the UN John Bolton must surely be counted among these skeptics, but he is hardly alone. It is this skepticism about the value of multilateral institutions in the era of globalization that helps explain why the Bush administration had no qualms about walking away from the Kyoto Protocol or the International Criminal Court, mechanisms designed to address gaps in the international order accentuated by the demise of the bipolar world order. The Bush administration would prefer to forge ad hoc coalitions of the willing—along the lines of the PSI—than to build up regional groups that might prove ineffective at "crunch time." This reluctance to invest in multilateral groups—a lack of enthusiasm that was vividly illustrated by Secretary of State Condoleezza Rice's failure to attend the ASEAN ministerial meeting in Vientiane in 2005 and President Bush's failure two years later to fulfill his promise to meet with the leaders of ASEAN—runs counter to the political culture of East Asia. The ability of the United States to elicit support or extract concessions "at crunch time" is directly proportional to the energy spent building close, cooperative, and cordial relations at times of relative ease.

The United States can be forgiven for not getting too excited about the formation of an East Asia community or the creation of the East Asia Summit. Given the lingering regional animosities among China, Japan, Korea, and Russia, and given the huge disparities between rich and poor, democratic and authoritarian regimes, the East Asia community hardly seems poised to form a cohesive block. Beyond efforts to reduce tariffs and non-tariff barriers to trade and promote regional integration (steps the United States welcomes), it is unclear whether an East Asia community can agree to an agenda for action. But the United States cannot afford to be complacent about East Asian regionalism or to neglect is own role in helping to shape or thwart the creation of an East Asia community. And if the United States remains reluctant to commit itself fully to the prospect of East Asia community building, it must at least take other practical steps to increase its capacity to address the new challenges it faces in East Asia and elsewhere.

ADVANCING US INTERESTS: A BLENDED APPROACH

The United States seems to have settled on a blended approach to advancing its core security and economic interests in East Asia, not only relying on traditional bilateral alliances (adapted to the post–Cold War world) but also working to develop effective ad hoc regional structures. The United States is not hostile to the creation of a more cohesive East Asia community, provided only that it does not attempt to exclude the United States. In fact, the United States has asked the members of APEC, ASEAN+3, the ARF, and other groups to work with them to advance common interests. This mixed strategy did not emerge quickly or without debate, and it remains unclear whether Washington will really throw its weight behind regional efforts to address East Asia's many challenges. At issue is whether the United States prefers to rely on bilateral alliances and ad hoc regional structures—both of which require constant nurturing—or whether it might be preferable to foster self-sustaining regional groups (even those that do not include the United States as a member) that could work on common challenges in parallel with US efforts and would not require constant US care and feeding. Also at issue is whether the United States is prepared to place its confidence in an East Asia community (one that explicitly does not include the United States as a "member") or whether the United States will judge that an East Asia community would tend either to be dominated by China or to advance an agenda at odds with core US interests.

Despite the demise of the Soviet Union and the end of the Cold War, the dominant analytical framework used by Washington to assess the future of the East Asian region and to reorient its alliances remains the balance-of-power theory. Many analysts have predicated their policy prescriptions on traditional zero-sum terms. As Aaron Friedberg, a former adviser to Vice President Cheney, put it in 2001, "Asia's future will resemble Europe's past; that it will be marked, in other words, by competitive great power politics, shifting alliances, costly arms races, periodic crises, and occasional wars."[4] Even those scholars or government officials emphasizing the positive trends toward regional integration usually concede that realpolitik and balance-of-power theory will

---

4. Aaron L. Friedberg, "Introduction," in *Strategic Asia: Power and Purpose*, ed. Richard J. Ellings and Aaron L. Friedberg (Seattle: National Bureau of Asian Research, 2001), 7.

best predict the complex patterns of interstate behavior in East Asia.[5] Given this reality, the United States is not going to abandon its bilateral alliances any time soon. But 9/11, avian influenza, the 2004 tsunami, and even global warming all graphically illustrate the need for those bilateral alliances to adapt to changing threats and for bilateral arrangements to be complemented by regional mechanisms to address emerging transnational challenges.

ALLIANCES IN TRANSITION: EXTENDED BILATERALISM

In fact, the United States *is* working to reconfigure its alliances so they may coexist with, and even support or complement, multilateral organizations. The United States understands that the post–Cold War world is marked by challenges that defy easy unilateral or bilateral solutions. The resilience of America's reconfigured bilateral alliances appears to defy the expectations of scholars such as Rajan Menon, who forecast in 2003 what he considered to be an inevitable outcome of the post–Cold War era: the obsolescence of US-led alliances in the absence of a clear organizing principle from which nations forge security partnerships.[6] According to Menon, absent the overarching threat of the Soviet Union or the emergence of a comparable villain, US bilateral alliances would whither. In fact, the ability of the United States to adapt its alliances to new roles and missions seems to confirm the view of Robert Scalapino that effective management of the challenges of East Asia will require a blend of balance-of-power and concert-of-power approaches.

Far from becoming obsolete, the US-Japan alliance, for instance, appears to be enjoying new life in new areas. The revised Guidelines for Japan-US Defense Cooperation allow for such previously unforeseen developments as the provision of Japanese logistical support for Operation Enduring Freedom (Afghanistan) and the application of the allies' acquisition and cross-servicing agreement to US and Japanese troops serving in Iraq and to tsunami relief efforts in Indonesia. The US-Japan alliance is today better positioned to address shared global

---

5. Amitav Acharya, "A Concert of Asia?" *Survival* 41, no. 3 (Autumn 1999): 84–101; Josh Kurlantzik, "Is East Asia Integrating?" *Washington Quarterly* 24, no. 4 (Autumn 2001).
6. Rajan Menon, "The End of Alliances," *World Policy Journal* 20, no. 2 (Summer 2003).

concerns and respond to nontraditional security threats, and a similar process is underway for the US-ROK alliance.

Some influential backers of the US-Japan alliance (including former Deputy Secretary of State Richard Armitage) have even called for broadening the alliance to make room for trilateral cooperation with China.[7] Forging such trilateral cooperation is considered important not only to address issues such as maritime security and nonproliferation but also to set the stage for a style of East Asian regionalism that will not jeopardize US interests.

In sum, US *exclusive* bilateral alliances in Asia appear to be giving way to *extended* bilateralism, designed to complement the growth of multilateral institutions and East Asia's tightening web of interdependence.[8] US alliances are being transformed from threat-based arrangements to interest-based partnerships. In essence, the United States' network of bilateral alliances seems likely to be extended and integrated, building on common interests and common values to complement and supplement multilateral institutions. Rather than competing with the institutions of regional and global governance that are a response to "the vacuum of power that occurs with increased interdependence and interaction among political communities,"[9] these new bilateral alliances "version 2.0" will accommodate a range of interests among the various regional players in East Asia and could help provide structure where there is no obvious supranational governing body.

Admiral Dennis Blair, former combatant commander of US Pacific Command, concurs with this shift away from a zero-sum balance of power mentality, arguing for "enriched bilateralism" that involves other regional powers as active participants. Blair sees these enriched bilateral alliances as steppingstones to genuine, effective multilateral institutions.[10] The TCOG (Trilateral Coordination and Oversight Group)

---

7. Richard Armitage and Joseph Nye, *The US-Japan Alliance in 2020: Getting Asia Right* (Washington DC: Center for Strategic and International Studies, 2007).

8. William Tow, "Assessing Bilateralism as a Security Phenomenon: Problems of Under-Assessment and Application" (working paper, Hawaii International Conference on Social Sciences, June 2003), as cited in *Alliance Diversification & the Future of the US-Korean Security Relationship*, ed. Charles Perry and James Schoff (Cambridge, MA: Institute of Foreign Policy Analysis, 2004).

9. Dan Oberg (conference paper, Global Governance Conference, Institute for International Policy Studies, Tokyo, October 2006).

10. Dennis Blair and John Hanley, "From Wheels to Webs: Reconstructing Asia-Pacific Security Arrangements," *Washington Quarterly* 24, no. 1 (Winter 2001).

process and the Six-Party Talks themselves are examples of the enriched bilateralism contemplated by Blair. Former Assistant Secretary of State James Kelly has testified before Congress that the Bush administration hopes the Six-Party Talks might evolve into an effective regional security forum, an idea that President Bush officially embraced at the 2006 APEC summit.

ECONOMIC INTEGRATION AND FREE TRADE AGREEMENTS

In the economic sphere, the United States is closely monitoring efforts of East Asian states to promote regional economic integration and perhaps form a cohesive economic unit or trading regime comparable to NAFTA. Washington is alert to any effort that might have the result of excluding the United States from the world's most dynamic economic region and wants to preserve its influence through the international financial institutions it helped to create and still leads.

The impetus for greater Asian economic integration flowed out of the 1997 Asian financial crisis and the failure of the International Monetary Fund or other international financial institutions to respond deftly to the emerging crisis or to deal effectively and compassionately with its aftermath. The United States blocked Malaysian and Japanese efforts to form an East Asian Economic Caucus and an Asian Monetary Fund, respectively, during the East Asian financial crisis—moves still remembered (and resented) by many East Asian states, particularly Thailand. In the wake of the collapse of the Asian Monetary Fund idea, the leaders of the ASEAN states met with the leaders of China, Japan, and South Korea in Malaysia in 1997 to see what might be done to forge closer cooperation among Asian states to promote economic stability and prevent unregulated capital flows. This first ASEAN+3 meeting led to the "Chiang Mai Initiative" in 2000, a network of currency swap arrangements designed to prevent a recurrence of the "Asian contagion."

The Asian financial crisis was a turning point in the quest for an East Asia community, providing a clear rationale for greater collective capacity to address a variety of economic challenges and promote mutually beneficial trade relations. But it is against this landscape of growing integration that regional rivalries also play out. Beijing's initiative to create a China-ASEAN FTA and Japan's interest in establishing an East Asia economic partnership agreement encompassing 16 countries, including ASEAN, Japan, China, South Korea, Australia, New Zealand, and India, reflect a competition for regional influence and leadership. The Bush administration countered by proposing a Free Trade Area of the Asia Pacific (FTAAP) at the APEC summit in 2006. An APEC-wide FTA would become the United States' largest FTA and would mark a departure from past US practice in Asia.

The notion of an APEC-wide FTA was a clever expansive countermove to narrower Chinese and Japanese proposals, but from the moment they floated FTAAP as an idea, senior members of the Bush administration must surely have known that it stood little chance of becoming reality. The obstacles were obvious, beginning with the institutional weakness of APEC itself. US support for, and reliance upon, APEC has been variable. At times, Washington has looked to APEC to drive forward regional trade liberalization, but at other times it has all but abandoned the economic agenda in favor of counterterrorism or other security priorities. Even if the members of APEC could negotiate an FTA, and even if APEC could somehow summon the institutional strength to implement such an accord, it is far from certain that the US Congress would ever bless a deal that probably would require the United States to abandon massive agricultural subsidies and include China in an FTA despite deep US concerns about product safety, intellectual property protection, and human rights in China. The proposal, therefore, is best understood as a US chess move to prevent the creation of any trading block that might put it at a disadvantage. Indeed, the more significant move on trade by the United States in 2006 was the signing of the US-ROK FTA, a bilateral accord designed to lock the United States into the region and counter efforts by China and the European Union to lure Korea away from the United States.

Multilateralism and the China Factor

Paradoxically, the emergence of China as a great power—reaching out to its Asian neighbors and increasingly active globally—is both a driver and an impediment to US support for an East Asia community. An East Asia community would at first blush appear to offer a useful hedge against any Chinese expansionist ambitions. At the same time, some fear that the creation of an East Asia community could magnify China's influence by giving it a community to dominate.

The appropriate US strategy toward China is the subject of much debate in Washington, although in truth the overall course of US-China relations has not deviated far from the path of engagement over the past 35 years. A few Cold Warriors continue to advocate containment, despite the inappropriate parallels to the Soviet Union and the sheer impossibility of containing 1.3 billion Chinese who are intent on restoring China to a position of global prominence. Some strategists envision a US-China "condominium" in East Asia, with separate spheres of influence designed to avoid entanglements. This notion seems hopelessly unrealistic given the reality of US global engagement and Washington's mistrust of Beijing's strategic intentions, to say nothing of the issue of Taiwan and its security. A few years ago the Rand Corporation offered up a strategy of *congagement*, a sort of "strategic hash" of policies drawn from containment and engagement that accurately captured the ambivalence that many Americans feel about China's rise without offering a truly compelling vision for what to do about it.[11] More recently, the Bush administration articulated the concept of China as a "responsible stakeholder." This update on Nixonian engagement clearly articulated the US desire that China become a responsible member of the international community but did not explicitly endorse the concept of an East Asia community of which China would necessarily be a major part. Most recently, the Council on Foreign Relations offered up a strategy of *integration*, blending three elements: *engaging* China on issues of mutual concern, *weaving* China into a web of regional and global institutions, and *balancing* China's military power.[12] The Council on Foreign Relations China Task Force explicitly endorsed paying greater attention to ASEAN, the ARF, and APEC and called on the United States to appoint an ambassador for ASEAN affairs and to sign the Treaty of Amity and Cooperation (and thus become eligible to attend the East Asia Summit).

Hopefully, the US response to China's rise will avoid the characteristics of the Cold War and will not repeat the errors of a previous era by

---

11. Zalmay Khalilzad, "Congage China," *RAND Issue Paper* IP-187 (1999), available online at www.rand.org/pubs/issue_papers/IP187/IP187.html.
12. Council on Foreign Relations, *US-China Relations: An Affirmative Agenda, A Responsible Course* (Task Force co-chairs: Carla Hills and Dennis Blair; project director: Frank Jannuzi) (New York: Council on Foreign Relations, 2007).

attempting to carve up East Asia into competing spheres of Chinese, Japanese, and US influence. China's emergence on the world stage is not a zero-sum game for the United States and its friends and allies. To the contrary, China's development can be a powerful force for good provided only that it is accompanied over the next three decades, as it has been for most of the past three decades, by growing Chinese adherence to international norms in the areas of security, trade, and human rights.

An excellent way to help ensure that China does indeed become a responsible stakeholder is to foster the development of an East Asia community that embodies the values that the United States at its best has championed at home and abroad: peaceful settlement of disputes, open markets, democracy, and respect for human rights. The creation of such an East Asia community would be a great boon to the United States, even if the United States were not a formal member of it, provided only that the community was constructed to be "open" rather than "closed." It is possible that such a community might emerge even without active US involvement and encouragement. But given the large number of competing regional structures—ASEAN, ASEAN+3, APEC, and the East Asia Summit—it makes sense for the United States to prioritize its efforts and to invest resources and energy into those structures best suited to meet its security and economic needs. Where necessary, as with the Six-Party Talks, the United States may still turn to ad hoc arrangements. But over the long haul, Washington's interests will be better served by the emergence of an integrated East Asia community that is self-sustaining and capable of tackling meaningful tasks, from responding to unanticipated financial shocks to curbing the threat of proliferation of weapons of mass destruction and promoting regional peace and security.

Clearly, the United States is not yet prepared to put its faith in the emerging, largely untested, East Asian regional organizations. For the foreseeable future it will continue to rely primarily on bilateral alliances to safeguard its vital interests in the region. But it would appear that the exclusive bilateralism that has been the hallmark of America's hub-and-spokes security arrangements is not well suited to the security challenges of the 21st century. And bilateral FTAs offer only a partial solution to the possibility that East Asia might form a trading block that would disadvantage the United States. Indeed, some have argued that bilateral arrangements and even regional agreements run counter to the spirit of truly open trade that is the goal of the WTO.[13]

As time goes by, the United States seems poised to embrace regionalism in East Asia, first as part of a mixed strategy and perhaps eventually as a genuine alternative to the bilateral alliances forged during the Cold War. There is some evidence that the United States is already moving in this direction. After 9/11, the United States looked to APEC to forge a regional consensus on how best to thwart Islamic radicalism. To address modern transnational crimes like drug running and trafficking in persons, the United States has created the International Law Enforcement Academy in Thailand. To rein in North Korea's nuclear ambitions, the United States worked with China to create the Six-Party Talks. Other new regional organizations appear to be an inevitable and appropriate response to the forces of globalization, economic interdependence, and nontraditional transnational security threats. But ultimately such ad hoc responses require a lot of work to sustain. It would be preferable for the nations of East Asia to forge an effective community capable of responding to the myriad threats that will inevitably challenge the maintenance of regional peace and stability. The nations and peoples of East Asia will have to decide the precise architecture of the East Asia community. Already, there has been much discussion of the issue, and perhaps the East Asia Summit will provide a forum for further strategic dialogue on the topic.

At Oxford University, and at my own *alma mater* of Yale, the dons on occasion dine at "High Table," where they discuss the great issues of the day (or their latest golf exploits, depending on the mood). President Bush (a Yale man) will not sign the Treaty of Amity and Cooperation, a necessary prerequisite for membership in the East Asia Summit. But the next US president probably will sign the treaty, even if he or she cannot get it ratified by the Senate. The next president will want the United States to have a seat at the high table of East Asia, if only to survey the scene and enjoy a good meal. Future US administrations will likely lead America to play a more constructive role in East Asia community building if only to ensure that the United States' position as a global leader is not compromised by its own neglect.

---

13. Jagdish Bhagwati, "The Consensus for Free Trade among Economists—Has it Frayed?" (lecture before the WTO, October 8, 2007), available online at www.wto.org/english/news_e/news07_e/bhagwati_oct07_e.htm.

9

Cooperation in Global Governance among East Asia, North America, and Europe: A European Perspective

KARL KAISER

A functioning and encompassing system of global governance has remained humanity's unfulfilled goal, although such governance already works to a degree in certain sectors. At the same time, a multitude of forces oriented toward that goal are caught in a never-ending process of progress and setbacks. Regionalism is one of the developments that have contributed to better governance in restricted geographical areas, and in doing so—for example, by advancing peace in a region—it has improved the chances for better global governance. Similarly, cooperation among regions can potentially contribute to global governance. The cooperation between North America and Europe was a decisive factor in the international politics of the second half of the last century and significantly affected global governance. Given the rise of Asia in recent decades, its increasing weight in world politics, as well as its growing regionalism and successful cooperation with North America and Europe, the question arises as to how these developments have affected the prospects for and evolution of global governance.

The Contemporary International Context

Compared with the world of the 1970s, a time when the bipolar structure of the Cold War created relative stability and when the first efforts were being made to systematically analyze the relations and possibilities for improved cooperation between Asia, Europe, and North America,[1] today's world is infinitely more volatile. The notion of "governance" is itself the product of this new era in which established institutions no longer adequately function, requiring that politicians and scholars seek new ways of regulating politics that take into account the emerging forces and structures of the contemporary world.

Though it can never be totally ruled out, the danger of large-scale war has practically disappeared, and the focus of security has shifted to internal war, ethnic cleansing, terrorism, and asymmetric war. Many of these problems are now arising inside, or are emanating from, the growing number of failed states. All three regions are deeply affected by these new security threats, which pose new challenges to their cooperation. The moves by NATO both to redefine its purpose and to increase its involvement in Afghanistan represent reactions to these changes and significantly expand the geographic focus of an originally Euro-Atlantic grouping into Western Asia.

The possibility of terrorists with access to weapons of mass destruction creates a nightmare scenario that must be taken seriously by every single state in the three regions. The threat of proliferation also poses grave problems, as the international regime designed to prevent the spread of nuclear weapons is in serious crisis—a crisis that may even usher in the demise of the Nonproliferation Treaty (NPT). Moreover, a nuclear-armed Iran or North Korea would have profoundly destabilizing effects on their regions, potentially unleashing regional arms races. It will not be possible to uphold the international nonproliferation regime and put an end to the nuclear weapons programs of North Korea and Iran unless the major powers in all three regions are willing to contribute to this goal.

---

1. The Trilateral Commission, a nongovernmental discussion group of intellectuals, politicians, business leaders, and journalists, was launched in 1973 as the first forum to analyze and promote cooperation among the three regions through meetings and publications. (For further information, see www.trilateral.org.)

Meanwhile, the situation in the Middle East appears to have become more volatile than ever: the war in Iraq has turned into a conflict that could inflame the entire region; Iran threatens to go nuclear; and the radical forces of Hamas and of Hezbollah, which it supports, are gaining ground. Needless to say, the Israeli-Palestinian conflict remains unresolved. Any escalation of these conflicts could disrupt oil exports, which would hit particularly hard at those countries in Asia, like China and India, that are desperately in need of rising imports for their development strategies. Though the main responsibility and potential for contribution to a solution lies with the United States and—to a lesser degree—with Europe rather than with Asia, all regions would suffer from a disruption of oil supplies.

All three regions have been profoundly affected by the rise of transnational relations and globalization, which have dramatically increased not only openness, interconnectivity, and interdependence but also vulnerability to forces from outside, be they terrorists, criminals, or financial speculation. The ensuing mutual dependency in solving problems stands in stark contrast to the prevailing concepts of classical state sovereignty (the Westphalian model) and territoriality. All three regions—but Asia in particular—will have to adapt their thinking, policies, and instruments to the new realities existing both within and between the regions.

At the same time, all three regions will have to face the severe, if not catastrophic, consequences of global warming. The divisive question of how to allocate the considerable costs of countermeasures will pose a major challenge to their ability to cooperate. Their capacity will be strained even further by the internal economic problems that a number of countries will encounter as a result of their aging populations.

It is also apparent that the future of relations among the three regions has to be considered in the context of a general weakening of multilateral rules and institutions that have been unable to deal effectively with many of the world's contemporary problems, such as ethnic cleansing, terrorism, or nonproliferation. Although the unilateralism practiced by the George W. Bush administration has contributed to this state of affairs, it is by no means solely responsible; the behavior of other powers and the inadequacy of institutional structures have played at least an equal role.

EAST ASIAN REGIONALISM AS SEEN FROM EUROPE

As the global system has evolved in this new era, the landscape of East Asia has shifted in fundamental ways. One major development in recent years is the increasing integration within East Asia as a region, which has accompanied the growth of prosperity throughout the area. However, a number of internal challenges exist that must be overcome if deeper and more substantive integration is to proceed with success.

Nationalism

While Europeans are always impressed by the extraordinary economic progress and the market integration in East Asia, they are also struck by the growing chauvinism and national stereotyping and the continuous and substantial arms buildup, which are reminiscent of experiences in Europe in the 20th century that proved to be precursors to war. Another parallel to Europe is the return of history as an issue in public discourse, particularly between China, Japan, and South Korea. But, whereas in Europe shared history became a driving force for reconciliation and integration, it remains a source of tension and antagonism in Asia.

Nowhere can this be seen as clearly as in the relations between the two biggest powers in the region, China and Japan. Their economic relations—trade, investment, outsourcing, exchange of know-how, and travel between the countries—have never been as advanced as they are today, and yet their political relations are at a very low point. Both countries see each other as rivals and view the other side's military buildup with great suspicion. Nationalist incidents directed at the other country have contributed to a further deterioration of relations.

One problem is that nationalism has been instrumentalized by the political class in both countries, though more intensely in China, where it follows a longer history of state-sponsored "patriotism" that has focused on Japan as its target. This "top-down" process is quite different from experiences in Europe after World War II. There, the "bottom-up" process was driven by a widespread desire for reconciliation in order to overcome the heritage of war and it converged with a "top-down" process by the political elites, who cooperated across frontiers to ensure that nationalism would not get out of hand and endanger their new venture into integration. If China and Japan could play the role that France and

Germany once played in Europe, leading the process of reconciliation and constructing a new Europe, they could turn around a development that has threatened the extraordinary achievements made by East Asia during the last decades.[2] But this presupposes a deliberate decision by the leadership to pursue such a path. Prime Minister Shinzo Abe's visit to Beijing in 2006 successfully arrested a negative trend but has not yet produced the kind of breakthrough that the two countries and the region need.

The Demographic Challenge

As the populations in China and Japan—two of the most populous countries of East Asia—continue to age, the workforce-to-pensioner ratio will worsen dramatically. By 2020, China will have more than 400 million pensioners over the age of 65. The welfare state systems of both countries will have to absorb the enormous costs of this shift, though Japan occupies a much better position as a wealthier country and a developed welfare state. Energy and resources will have to be redirected toward domestic politics. In China, this could assume crisis proportions with unforeseeable consequences for social stability. In both countries, pressure is likely to grow to reallocate resources away from foreign policy, for example from development aid or the military.

The consequences of these changes for regionalism are hard to predict. Not unlike the case in Europe, as a country like Japan "ages," the ensuing problems enhance the rationale for a more liberal regime for the free movement of labor and immigration. In order to be managed properly, both would require a minimum of regulatory arrangements at the regional level to deal, for example, with the movement of Southeast Asian caregivers into Japan. At the same time, immigration and foreign workers raise difficult issues of social and political integration and face considerable difficulties due to the growing public aversion to the influx of foreigners in many countries.[3]

---

2. One example could be the Franco-German Youth Office that Konrad Adenauer and Charles de Gaulle created in 1963, which conducts exchange programs that to date have brought together 7 million young people to meet within structured environments.
3. See, for example, Pew Research Center, *World Publics Welcome Global Trade—But Not Immigration: 47-Nation Pew Global Attitudes Survey, October 4* (Washington DC: Pew Research Center, 2007).

The Unrealized Potential of Economic Interdependence

Integration in East Asia has made enormous progress. Originally driven in large part by Japanese investment and aid, integration soon developed its own dynamism, reinforced by globalization and the growth of China and the "Little Tigers." Intraregional trade amounts to 54 percent of the members' trade, thus approaching the rate of the European Union (EU; 60 percent). Though China attracts about 60 percent of foreign direct investment (FDI) in East Asia (much of it from Japan), there is a regionwide system of cross-investment that reinforces what the high rate of intraregional trade reflects: complex networks of outsourcing and a system of internationally managed production that extend throughout the region.

Though economic integration increasingly ties the countries of East Asia together and amplifies their mutual dependency—as the 1997 crisis demonstrated—institutions with binding arrangements that manage this interdependence have failed to follow. As a former secretary-general of ASEAN observed, "Because ASEAN has few binding agreements and lacks a regional authority to enforce compliance with them, regional economic integration and closer ASEAN cooperation are almost totally dependent on national policy decisions and on the commitment of leaders to the region."[4] Although ASEAN has taken steps to promote integration and cooperation in many areas, it has still not been able to develop its full potential because of its structure of governance.

This situation could change following the implementation of the ASEAN Charter, which was based on the December 2006 recommendations of the Eminent Persons Group on the ASEAN Charter[5] and was adopted in November 2007. In the past, it was often asserted that ASEAN could not become an institution like the EU, but the structure of the charter moves it in that direction and even shows some similarities to the EU. Besides giving it a legal personality, ASEAN is to have an "ASEAN Council" at the top (like the European Council of the EU); three ministerial-level councils to oversee the ASEAN Security Community, the ASEAN Economic Community, and the ASEAN Socio-Cultural Community; as well as a single market with free movement of goods,

---

4. Rodolfo C. Severino, *South East Asia in Search of an ASEAN Community* (Singapore: ISEAS, 2006), 377.
5. See ASEAN, *Report of the Eminent Persons Group on the ASEAN Charter* (Jakarta: ASEAN, 2006), 49.

ideas, and skilled labor (although not all labor). A strong secretariat is to give advice and monitor compliance.

Not all of the more ambitious new ideas proposed for the ASEAN Charter by the Eminent Persons Group were adopted, nor is it likely that a community similar to the EU, with its institutions, sovereignty transfer, and common currency, will emerge in the foreseeable future. Nevertheless, the general undertaking is likely to shift the geopolitical landscape in Asia by creating an institutionalized group of smaller and medium-sized states with an identity and organizational capacity of its own that would extend its activities to security and foreign policy and would strengthen the negotiating weight of this group vis-à-vis Japan, China, India, and others. The implementation of the ASEAN Charter is likely to improve the chances for better management of regional interdependence and would also create a more effective player within the Asia-Europe Meeting (ASEM) and other Asian-European activities.

Comparing Regionalism in East Asia and Europe

Though regionalism in East Asia has made considerable progress, it has not reached the level of Western Europe's integration—if indeed it ever will—because a number of supporting forces have been absent or different in East Asia. Foremost is the shared history of wars, which in Europe created a powerful movement that declared "never again," resulting in a convergence of elite and popular opinion to establish a radically different basis for relations among the nations of Europe. This desire for reconciliation became the driving force in overcoming the patterns of the past, resulting in a shared conviction that each nation had to honestly face the failures and wrongdoings in its history.

Despite all the suffering that Japan's war with China and its occupation of Korea caused, those events still do not compare with the endless cycle of wars in Europe, nor are they comparable to the millions of deaths and widespread destruction that the European wars engendered. And despite the political forces in Japan, China, and Korea that have sought a new beginning in their relations, and the numerous apologies offered by Japanese spokesmen, a "never again" movement with the power of the European effort has never arisen. The failure of Japan as a body politic to thoroughly break with its past as Germany did after World War II has contributed to this state of affairs.[6]

A second factor that played a great role in advancing European integration—and that has been practically absent in East Asia—was the consistent support of the United States. It started with the Marshall Plan, which was granted on the condition that the Europeans themselves administer its implementation, thus giving impetus to European bureaucracies to cooperate for the first time and to foster regional economic interaction. Japan's early official development assistance in Asia in a way created a common economic space in East Asia, but it was a system organized around Japan as the hub and it lacked the political and institutional framework that the Marshall Plan provided. Throughout the postwar period, the United States relentlessly supported the European integration effort, intervening diplomatically when necessary and supporting those political forces in European politics that favored European unity. Only under the administration of George W. Bush were doubts raised (on the neoconservative side) as to whether it was wise to support the emergence of a "rival" to the United States who could sometimes thwart Washington's policies.[7] But in its second term, the administration reconfirmed the continuity of American support for European integration, and George W. Bush demonstratively was the first US president to visit the EU institutions in Brussels.

The Soviet threat, both as an ideological and a security challenge, provided a powerful additional reason for the Europeans to integrate. To be sure, NATO was the main instrument organizing European participation in an anti-Soviet alliance, but the political atmosphere of the founding years of European unification was dominated by an all-pervasive perception of a Soviet threat that extended into the heart of Europe with a vast Soviet military force being deployed in East Germany and around Berlin. This threat provided an additional reason to pool European resources and acted as the glue to help mend divisions among the members.

---

6. See, for example, Karl Kaiser, "European History 101 for Japan and China," *INTERNATIONALE POLITIK* (global edition) Summer 2006: 90–97. To be sure, the "never again" concept has a somewhat different meaning for the Central European countries that joined the EU in 2004. For them, the experience of and protection against a revival of communism has been a defining motive for their membership, which partly explains why they are more reluctant to transfer sovereignty than the "older" members.
7. See, for example, Jeffrey Cimbalo, "Saving NATO from Europe," *Foreign Affairs* 83, no. 6 (November/December 2004): 111–120.

The Soviet threat existed in East Asia as well but was significantly weaker for military and geographical reasons. It helped to create a system of bilateral security relations with the United States as a hub. An attempt to create a kind of counterpart to NATO with the establishment of the Southeast Asia Treaty Organization in 1954 never got off the ground and was finally abandoned in 1977.[8] The ASEAN Regional Forum always remained modest in its scope, but hopefully the ASEAN Security Community within the new ASEAN Charter will give more content to East Asian regionalism in the security field.

Finally, despite all the cultural differences, for example between Protestant Scandinavia and Catholic Southern Europe, the internal diversity within Europe was much less distinct than that of East Asia. Very soon after 1945, the Western European countries were democracies, followed the rule of law, and shared the tradition of basic human rights. (Portugal and Spain joined this group only later.) In East Asia, several countries have only recently adopted the rule of law and democracy, and to this day the region is characterized by a considerable diversity of regimes and political traditions. The shared basis in values and institutional traditions in Europe greatly facilitated, and was indeed the prerequisite for, an agreement on the institutional structure of the European Community, a partial transfer of sovereignty, as well as the formation of Europe-wide political parties in the European Parliament.

This is not to say that in the absence of the conditions that favored European integration East Asian regionalism will not be able to advance significantly. The extraordinary economic integration in the region creates dependencies, which in turn put growing pressure on both the elites and on mass opinion on two levels. First, institutional arrangements become necessary to give direction to the process, to avoid negative fallout, and to maximize the advantages of integration. Second, the success of integration creates a growing interest not to let political crises, be they caused by nationalism or differences in interests, get out of hand and threaten the achievements of decades. Moreover, many of the contemporary global problems, notably terrorism, proliferation, global warming, and economic security, should provide powerful incentives to cooperate in East Asia. In all of these cases, however, the "top-down" process among political elites must be complemented by a "bottom-up"

8. Amitav Acharya, "Why Is There No NATO in Asia? The Normative Origins of Asian Multilateralism," Working Paper Series No. 05-05 (2005), Weatherhead Center for International Affairs, Harvard University.

process that involves the peoples of the region. In this respect as well, the European experience provides a good model for East Asia.

GLOBAL CHALLENGES AND REGIONAL RESPONSES

While the efforts at regional cooperation in East Asia must overcome a number of internal problems, global challenges such as nonproliferation, shifts in the nature of international security, and global warming in turn have critical implications for regionalism. They also make both regional and interregional cooperation more imperative.

The Nonproliferation Regime, Iran, and North Korea

The future of the nonproliferation regime will be decided both by what happens to the general principles of the international regime and by the two cases of Iran and North Korea. Unless the major powers of the three regions cooperate, the regime is unlikely to survive.

At the general level of the international regime, it is imperative that the commitments made on the occasion of the renewal of the NPT in 1995 be implemented. In this regard, the United States is called upon to abandon its opposition to the Comprehensive Test Ban Treaty and a cut-off agreement on fissile materials (also to help induce India and Pakistan to follow suit). Moreover, the regime must be strengthened by giving the International Atomic Energy Agency better means to enforce its controls and by developing new approaches to internationalize the nuclear fuel supply in order to avoid national enrichment and reprocessing of spent fuel. All major powers, and in particular the five permanent members of the UN Security Council, must contribute to this goal.

A peaceful approach to induce Iran to renounce nuclear weapons will fail if China and Russia—possibly concerned about their commercial links with Iran and, in the case of China, its oil supply—are unwilling to support meaningful sanctions should Iran fail to comply with the UN Security Council's decision that Iran forgo national enrichment. Here, as on other issues of nonproliferation, China will hopefully act to an increasing extent as a stakeholder in international stability—as it did in the case of North Korea and as behooves such a great power—and not give precedence to its short-term economic interests.

In the case of North Korea, complete success in having the country renounce nuclear weapons is also only achievable if the five countries negotiating with it remain united in their purpose. This requires in particular a continuation of China's constructive and helpful role, the continued willingness of the United States to deal with North Korea bilaterally, South Korea's engagement in opening up the North economically, and Japan's active support. Should more far-reaching agreements that reward the regime by economic means be concluded, then the EU should contribute in the interest of global stability, as it did once before on a modest level in the case of the Korean Peninsula Energy Development Organization (KEDO).

International Security

In an interconnected world with relatively open borders, threats to security can spread globally and affect every region and country. Terrorist extremism is a global threat and has struck countries in all three regions. Its transnational character necessitates intergovernmental cooperation between intelligence services, police, customs authorities, and others. All three regions have made significant progress, though none of them can claim to have reached the desired level. Here the classical concept of sovereignty still acts as a brake. Similarly, interregional cooperation is only in its initial phase, with European–North American cooperation being the most advanced.

Dealing with the roots of terrorist extremism is at once the most difficult and the most time-consuming part of fighting terrorism. All countries can contribute in their own way to combat this common threat by promoting a dialogue with moderate Islam at home and abroad. They can help to isolate the extremist minority by addressing the religious, social, and economic issues that drive young men to become terrorists. Within East Asia, Indonesia and Malaysia, as moderate Muslim countries and democracies, should play a leadership role in such an effort. Moreover, any support given by East Asian (in particular Muslim) countries to the efforts of the Middle East Quartet to overcome the Israeli-Palestinian conflict would be helpful, since that would take away one of the factors that has animated Muslim extremism.

Failed states are one of the most momentous problems in the modern world of global security; they cause widespread human suffering and can become havens for terrorists and criminals who threaten others. Afghanistan provides the most important case in point. In the context of a UN mandate, NATO—as a North American–European alliance—has chosen Afghanistan as the focal point for redefining its very purpose by innovatively combining military and civilian means to reconstruct the country, rebuild institutions, and defeat the insurgents. A return of the Taliban would be as much a threat to Asia as it would be to North America and Europe. Defeating the Taliban is therefore in the interest of global security, and Asian countries should contribute substantially, as Japan has done.

From a European perspective, East Asia has a special responsibility with regard to North Korea and Myanmar because the repressive character of these failing states, as well as the North Korean policy of exporting missiles and nuclear weapons technology, are matters of global concern.

Global Warming

Among all of the new problems facing the world today, the warming of the earth's atmosphere is truly global. As it progresses, it will have catastrophic consequences in the countries of all three regions. Although the United States is the world's largest emitter of greenhouse gases, it has so far refused to make even small changes in its wasteful policies. Lagging behind Europe and Japan, the United States could potentially make a tremendous contribution to a global issue—and one that also affects it enormously at home—if it were to revise its policy.

From a historical perspective, Europe and North America (and later Japan) have generated the overwhelming share of the globe's greenhouse gases during the last 150 years. But countries like China and India that therefore claim a right to first catch up with industrial development without undertaking costly countermeasures are not facing up to their global responsibility. Much can be done in this field through political intervention and without significant cost. Modern technologies are now available that are significantly more efficient at only marginal additional cost. It is in the self-interest of the industrialized and wealthy countries to transfer technologies and substantial fiscal means to help the developing world reduce their contribution to global warming.

The EU has chosen a regional path to commit the member countries to greenhouse gas reduction that even goes beyond the targets of the Kyoto Protocol. Though East Asia has not reached the same depth of regional integration that made the joint European approach possible, regional agreements on cooperating within ASEAN+3 should make sense as complementary action to global measures, given the high degree of economic integration and transnational investments.

TRILATERAL RELATIONS AND GLOBAL GOVERNANCE

The way the three regions—Europe, North America, and East Asia— interact will influence their impact on global governance. In this respect it must be noted that considerable differences in internal structure and strength exist among the respective relations between the trilateral areas. Of the three, the North American–European relationship is the strongest, while Asian-European relations are still the weakest.

The European–North American Relationship

North America and Europe today form a genuine security community, within which the use of force to resolve conflicts is reliably excluded. Its core is the North Atlantic Alliance that links North America and practically all of Western and Central Europe. The alliance is now redefining its purpose and has chosen an Asian country of global importance, Afghanistan, as the central focus of its new activities. At the same time, NATO is trying to establish partnerships with countries in the Asia Pacific area, including Japan, Australia, and New Zealand. The governments of NATO argue vis-à-vis their democratic publics that the alliance is acting under a UN mandate and that, by fighting terrorism and rebuilding a previously failed state, NATO is making an indispensable contribution to world order.

The EU and its far-reaching integration give additional weight to the European–North American relationship. EU security policy addresses the new transnational security threat as well and has evolved within the context of a division of labor with NATO. The EU increasingly plays a stabilizing role in the Balkans, once ravaged by war. Since the

149

EU provides more than half of the world's development assistance and has created a system of special relationships, dialogue forums, and aid systems with neighboring regions and associated countries, it also plays a major global role in the nonmilitary field.

The EU–North America relationship is equally strong in the economic area. Trade provided the initial starting point for the growth of an Atlantic economy. Today, however, its main basis is not trade, although that is strong and rising, but rather a growing share of mutual investment. This practice has created "deep integration," tying the economies together much more effectively than mere trade. Most of America's FDI (some 56 percent) still goes to Europe. In comparison, total US investment in China was just 23 percent of its investment in Belgium.[9] The Atlantic economy of today is comprised of a vast network of border-crossing activities, reflected in the fact that more than half of transatlantic trade is comprised of the internal trade of multinational companies.

As a result, the two regions have become the driving forces of global governance in the economic area, particularly in trade liberalization, although as shown in the Doha Round, other countries have become important forces as well. Another area of global importance where they have been particularly active is the protection of intellectual property rights, supported by other developed countries in Asia such as Japan and South Korea.

The Asian–North American Relationship

The Asian–North American relationship is by comparison somewhat weaker and even more diverse. It is based on a network of bilateral relations as well as linkages with regional forums in Asia that are relatively weak and nonbinding in character. These range from groupings like APEC, in which the United States takes part, to those like ASEAN, ASEAN+3, and the East Asia Summit, where the United States does not. The Six-Party Talks on North Korea are a special case and are of global importance since they are part of efforts to preserve the international nonproliferation regime.

---

9. Daniel S. Hamilton and Joseph P. Quinlan, eds., *Deep Integration. How Transatlantic Markets are Leading Globalization* (Washington DC: Center for Transatlantic Relations, 2005); Hamilton and Quinlan, *The Transatlantic Economy 2006* (Washington DC: Center for Transatlantic Relations, 2007).

Within the network of bilateral relations, the US-Japan alliance is central: flanked by other bilateral security arrangements, notably between the United States and South Korea, it has been the basis of stability in the region. With its naval presence and multitude of security agreements (including its support of Taiwan), the United States has provided a crucial and central element of Asia's stability and formed a protective roof under which economic relations could flourish.

On the economic side, the Asian–North American relationship is quite different from its European–North American counterpart. To be sure, there is an extraordinary and growing amount of economic interaction and mutual dependence, but compared with the transatlantic relationship, it is based more on trade and less on mutual investment. The extent of this relationship, of course, has deepened steadily with the rise of China and its commercial links with the United States.

Currency issues provide an additional dimension since China and Japan today hold huge foreign exchange reserves—notably US dollar reserves. China now holds the world's largest foreign exchange reserves, totaling US$1.2 billion.[10] China and Japan are America's main creditors today, thus creating an additional element of economic mutual dependence besides the trade relationship. Within the global governance system of currency management, sooner or later China is likely to take a seat at the table of the traditional G-3—the United States, Japan, and Europe.

The Asian-European Relationship

The Asian-European relationship is somewhat weaker than the two others but is catching up. Political contacts began with the ministerial meetings in the early 1970s between ASEAN and the European Economic Community (EEC) after commercial relations had steadily increased in the preceding years. ASEAN sought these contacts with the EEC, which was a successful regional organization and was the first to extend a much-appreciated official recognition to the Southeast Asian grouping. The contacts evolved into regular meetings, first discussing trade issues but later extending their scope to a broad spectrum of issues.

---

10. *Financial Times*, April 13, 2007, 6.

The relationship was deepened by the establishment in 1996 of a regular summit meeting, ASEM, comprised of the EU and ASEAN+3.[11]

ASEM has generated a multitude of meetings and consultations at various official levels and on many issues, and in the process it has forced the Asian side to develop common positions prior to the encounters, thus advancing their internal coordination. Yet, as noted in a recent report evaluating ASEM's first decade, it has also been criticized for not having fulfilled initial expectations and for not having "been successful in coordinating or harmonizing the interests of it partners efficiently vis-à-vis larger organizations and bodies."[12] Nevertheless, as the same report states, "The undertaking should be viewed in a long-term perspective." It is precisely the widespread sense of unexplored potential that generated the far-reaching proposals for an ASEAN Charter. The charter could significantly alter the Asian-European relationship by creating a well-organized and better-integrated Southeast Asian grouping that, together with China, Japan, and South Korea (and later possibly with India), could form a better-structured counterpart for the EU in their mutual dealings.

In the field of security, cooperation between Asia and Europe in combating terrorism has become increasingly necessary. Asian participation in NATO's activities in Afghanistan would be desirable in the future as a contribution to global stability. The creation of an ASEAN Security Community under the ASEAN Charter might even increase the capacity of the Southeast Asian nations to cooperate in such ventures.

The economic relationship between Asia and Europe has steadily deepened; the EU is now almost as important as the United States as a commercial partner with Asia. In 2005, the total trade of ASEAN+3 with the EU amounted to US$622 billion, compared with US$722 billion with the United States.[13] ASEAN had a net FDI influx of US$8.7 billion from the United States and US$7.1 billion from the EU. Not surprisingly, the somewhat conflictual issues in their relations are not very different

---

11. Michael Reiterer, *Asia-Europe. Do They Meet? Reflections on the Asia-Europe Meeting (ASEM)* (Singapore: Asia-Europe Foundation, 2002); Cesar de Prado, *Global Multi-Level Governance: European and East Asian Leadership* (Tokyo: United Nations University Press, 2007).

12. Japan Center for International Exchange (JCIE) and the University of Helsinki Network for European Studies, eds., *ASEM in its Tenth Year. Looking Back, Looking Forward. An Evaluation of ASEM in its First Decade and an Exploration of its Future Possibilities* (Tokyo: JCIE, 2006), 7.

13. The EU figure does not include Hong Kong.

from those between the United States and Asia: intellectual property rights, selective protectionism, ownership rights of investments, and currency exchange rates.

CONCLUSION

There are numerous areas in which the contribution of the three regions to global governance is indispensable. These include fighting terrorism (both defending against it and tackling its root causes); dealing with failed states (and stabilizing Afghanistan in particular); saving and strengthening the international nonproliferation regime and preventing Iran and North Korea from going nuclear; and reducing global warming.

Regionalism makes an important contribution to global governance. Its growth and the successful solution of its internal challenges are therefore of wider importance. That is also true of interregional cooperation, but in order to flourish it needs multilateral frameworks. At the center of all efforts to strengthen global governance must, therefore, be the attempt to stop the further deterioration of multilateralism that has occurred in recent years and, instead, to reinforce multilateral approaches and institutions.[14] In this respect, Asia, Europe, and other regions have disagreed with the unilateralism and the rejection of international regimes displayed by the US administration of George W. Bush. Interestingly, having experienced the failure of its policies, it came around in its second term to a more multilateral approach. In order to be successful at the global level, efforts to restore multilateralism must indeed include the world's most powerful country.

Strengthening multilateralism first and foremost means resuming the process of reforming the UN. Considerable progress has been made at the conceptual level, including the reports on "the responsibility to protect" and "human security." The recommendations of former UN Secretary-General Kofi Annan's High-Level Panel and his ensuing conclusions outline a sensible avenue for reforms. Seeing these recommendations through will be crucial in tackling the central issues of security for all three regions, namely addressing situations in which the

---

14. See also the summary of a Council for Asia-Europe Cooperation exercise in Karl Kaiser, ed., *Asia and Europe: The Necessity for Cooperation* (Tokyo: JCIE, 2004).

international community must deal with failed states, terrorists, and weapons of mass destruction. So far, there has been a great reluctance to draw any practical solutions from these proposals. It is up to the three regions, which have formidable intellectual, human, and economic resources, to transform these proposals into concrete policies.

Appendix

About the Contributors

JESUS P. ESTANISLAO chairs the Institute of Corporate Directors and the Institute for Solidarity in Asia, both in Manila. He has served in a wide range of private and public posts, including in the cabinet of President Corazon Aquino as secretary of finance (1990–1992) and as secretary of economic planning and director general of the National and Economic Development Authority (1989).

JAMES GANNON is executive director of the Japan Center for International Exchange (JCIE/USA) in New York.

CAROLINA G. HERNANDEZ is emeritus professor of political science at the University of the Philippines, Diliman, and founding president and chair of the board of directors of the Institute for Strategic and Development Studies. She has served in a wide range of governmental and nongovernmental posts, including as a presidential advisor in the cabinet of President Gloria Macapagal-Arroyo.

FRANK JANNUZI is a professional staff member for the US Senate Committee on Foreign Relations. He was a Hitachi International Affairs Fellow with the Council on Foreign Relations and has also worked for the US State Department's Bureau of Intelligence and Research.

KARL KAISER is director of the Transatlantic Relations Program at the Weatherhead Center for International Affairs and adjunct professor of public policy at the John F. Kennedy School of Government, both at Harvard University. A recipient of the Atlantic Award of NATO, he was a director of the German Council on Foreign Relations (DGAP) for three decades and has served as an advisor to numerous leaders, including Chancellors Willy Brandt and Helmut Schmidt.

ADAM P. LIFF is a research associate at JCIE and a MEXT research scholar affiliated with the University of Tokyo.

QIN YAQING is vice president and professor of international affairs at China Foreign Affairs University. He served on the resource team for the UN High Level Panel for Challenges, Threats, and Change (2003) and as special assistant to the Chinese eminent person for the China-ASEAN Eminent Persons Group (2005).

RIZAL SUKMA is deputy executive director of the Centre for Strategic and International Studies (CSIS) in Jakarta. He also chairs the International Relations Division of the Central Executive Board of Muhammadiyah, Indonesia's second largest Islamic organization, and served as a member of the Indonesian Ministry of Defense's National Committee on Strategic Defense Review.

HITOSHI TANAKA is a senior fellow at JCIE. Prior to joining JCIE in 2005, he held a range of high-ranking posts in Japan's Ministry of Foreign Affairs during his 36-year career as a diplomat, most recently as deputy minister for foreign affairs.

JUSUF WANANDI is a senior fellow at CSIS, Jakarta, which he helped found, and vice chair of the CSIS Foundation. He has served in a wide range of governmental and nongovernmental posts, including as a representative in the People's Consultative Assembly for four terms, and he currently chairs the Indonesian National Committee for the Pacific Economic Cooperation Council and the Council for Security Cooperation in the Asia Pacific. He is also president of *The Jakarta Post*, Indonesia's leading English-language newspaper.

TADASHI YAMAMOTO founded JCIE in 1970 and serves as the president. He also serves as the director of the Pacific Asia regional group of the Trilateral Commission, as well as of the UK-Japan 21st Century Group, the German-Japan Forum, the Korea-Japan Forum, and the Friends of the Global Fund, Japan.

About APAP and JCIE

ASIA PACIFIC AGENDA PROJECT

The Asia Pacific Agenda Project (APAP) is a multinational consortium of policy research organizations and academic institutions dedicated to strengthening networks and enhancing joint research and dialogue among institutions and intellectual leaders in the Asia Pacific. It also aims to train young scholars as future leaders by involving them in international policy-related research. The Japan Center for International Exchange (JCIE) and the consortium's other member institutions sponsor joint policy research projects and hold workshops, seminars, and an annual forum to discuss their research findings. This publication is the product of an APAP joint policy study.

JAPAN CENTER FOR INTERNATIONAL EXCHANGE

JCIE serves as the secretariat for APAP. Founded in 1970, it is one of the few independent, nongovernmental organizations in the field of international affairs in Japan. A nonprofit and nonpartisan organization, it conducts programs of exchange, research, and dialogue that bring together key figures from diverse sectors of society in Japan and overseas.

JCIE's activities are carried out in collaboration with organizations around the world, and it operates many of its programs in cooperation with its American affiliate, JCIE/USA, which is based in New York. JCIE creates opportunities for informed policy discussions; it does not take policy positions. It receives no government subsidies; rather funding comes from private foundation grants, corporate contributions, individual donations, and contracts.

Japan Center for International Exchange (JCIE/Japan)
www.jcie.or.jp

Japan Center for International Exchange, Inc. (JCIE/USA)
www.jcie.org

Index